I. BRONZE STATUETTE OF A CAROLINGIAN EMPEROR
Paris, Musée Carnavalet.

ROGER HINKS

CAROLINGIAN ART

LONDON
SIDGWICK & JACKSON, LTD.
1935

To

T. E. J.

PRINTED IN GREAT BRITAIN
BY R. & R. CLARK, LIMITED, EDINBURGH

CONTENTS

LIST OF ILLUSTRATIONS

The author is indebted to the Trustees of the British Museum, the Directors of the Bibliothèque Nationale, the Bibliothèque de l'Arsenal, the Musée Carnavalet, the Museo Nazionale in Rome, the Castello Sforzesco in Milan, the Staatliche Museen in Berlin, the Schnütgenmuseum in Cologne, and the Hessisches Landesmuseum at Darmstadt, and the Librarians of Corpus Christi College, Cambridge, the Bayerische Staatsbibliothek in Munich, the Universiteitsbibliotheek at Utrecht, and the Stadtbibliotheken at Frankfort, Leipzig, and Trier, for permission to reproduce objects in the care of those institutions; to the Deutscher Verein für Kunstwissenschaft, the Pegasus Press, and Prof. Gerhart Rodenwaldt; and to the firms of Alinari, Anderson, Bätz, Catala, Fleming, Giraudon, Paoletti, Rheinisches Bildarchiv, Stoedtner, and Tams for permission to use photographs of which they hold the copyright.

INTRODUCTION

THE history of medieval art in western Europe starts as an organic growth from the Carolingian Renascence at the end of the eighth century. Until that date the Christian narrative and didactic art of the Mediterranean world had never fused completely with the ornamental and non-representational art of the Celtic and Germanic north. This process took place during the ninth century in the workshops attached to the court of Charles the Great and his successors and in its dependent monasteries; and it is the object of this book to show how the antique tradition, itself the work of different races and ideals, was there interpreted by the Nordic imagination and refashioned to suit Nordic requirements.

The detailed history of Carolingian art has been worked out by authorities like Boinet, Goldschmidt, Köhler, Leitschuh, Merton, Rand, Schlosser, and Swarzenski; and my debt to their researches will be apparent on every page. These scholars have been mainly concerned with the regional development of Carolingian art and with the classification of the different schools of book-painters and ivory-carvers working at Aachen, Corbie, Metz, Reichenau, Rheims, Saint-Denis, St. Gall, Tours, and elsewhere. But in a book like this, intended for the general student of European art, it has seemed better not to insist on these geographical distinctions, and to concentrate rather upon the wider aspects of the problem, such as the relationship of Carolingian book-painting and ivory-carving to their late-antique prototypes, the formal aspects of the Nordic imagination, and the internal development of the Frankish aesthetic sense during the course of the ninth century. In particular, the connexion between Carolingian copy and late-antique model seems to me at once so important and so imperfectly understood that I have devoted about half the book to events that happened centuries before Charles the Great ever saw the light of day. The necessity for this will, I think, be obvious to anybody who follows the development of my analysis.

My grateful thanks are due to Mr. Francis Wormald, of the Department of MSS. at the British Museum, and to Dr. Walther Horn, of Heidelberg, for their kindness in reading my text in manuscript and proof and in making many useful suggestions and criticisms.

R. H.

CAROLINGIAN ART

A Study of Early Medieval Painting and Sculpture in Western Europe

CAROLINGIAN ART

PART ONE

THE ORIGINS OF MEDIEVAL ART IN WESTERN EUROPE

I

THE art of the Roman Empire, like its political structure, is a hybrid growth.[1] Its formal, intellectual, and emotional content is derived from very various sources; and it presents to the critical student of a later age a disconcertingly ambiguous appearance. His judgement of its value and its originality will depend upon the character and range of his interests. If he approaches it from an iconographical standpoint he will note the continuity and prevalence of Hellenistic themes, and will be inclined to doubt whether the Romans added anything of importance to the later Greek repertory of types and motifs. If he is concerned with strict morphological principles he will observe that the space-composition of Roman art follows methods invented long before in Egypt

[1] The most general treatment of Roman art is that of Wickhoff in the introduction of his work on the Vienna Genesis MS. (translated and revised by Mrs. Strong under the title of *Roman Art*); cf. also Strong, *Scultura romana*; *ead.*, *Art in Ancient Rome*; Koch, *Römische Kunst.* All these writers insist on the essential originality of Roman art. For a recent statement of the contrary view that the art of the Roman Empire is only the last phase of Greek art, see Toynbee, *The Hadrianic School: a Chapter in the History of Greek Art.*

and in Mesopotamia,[1] and logically implied in Hellenistic art, of which he will regard the Roman imperial style as the final stage. A historian, moreover, will note that when an artist's name is given in the Roman period, that name is generally Greek;[2] and an ethnologist will perceive a connexion between many of the commonest features of Roman decorative art and the symbols of Mazdaism and other ancient religions of the East.[3] On the other hand, those who believe that the true function of art is to give concrete expression to abstract ideas will be able to point to real advances in naturalistic portraiture, in the representation of historic events, and in the aesthetic exploitation of plant and animal life.

To decide between the merits of these claims and counter-claims is not easy. We have to make up our minds whether to treat Roman art as an original activity, or as the last phase of Greek art, or as the realisation in Mediterranean terms of ancient modes of visualising and rendering form inherited from the East. And if there is found to be some justification for all these points of view, we have to judge which standard of values is decisive, and, more specifically, what was the quality in Roman art that could account for its widespread and enduring popularity in the Middle Ages and the Renascence.

In dealing with so fundamental a problem we must take the widest possible view of Roman art. We must compare it with other Roman institutions. We must

[1] See Rodenwaldt in *JHS.*, liii. (1933), pp. 206 ff., with references to detailed discussions of the debt of Roman to oriental art.

[2] Cf. Overbeck, *Die antiken Schriftquellen*, nos. 2214 ff.

[3] E.g. Strzygowski, *Origin of Christian Church Art*, pp. 6 ff., and *passim*.

consider it as the monumental statement of the Roman world-idea. We must discover, in fact, what is the essentially Roman quality in Roman art. If its individual forms are Greek, its synthetic principles of Asiatic descent, and only its content is Roman, how has it succeeded in imposing itself upon the imagination of a posterity so differently endowed and situated? Why, for example, did Christianity entrust to Roman art the greatest of all missionary responsibilities? Why, moreover, did the Germanic founders of the medieval political order find themselves compelled to revive the Roman pictoral tradition as their chief method of visual propaganda?

The answer to all these questions is that the Roman tradition was the most comprehensive and the most efficient available. Just as the conception of a single world-order was Hellenistic in design but Roman in execution, so the ideal of a completely human art may have been imagined by the Greeks but was achieved by the Romans. It is their ability to realise in detailed fact the most ambitious projects of the political mind that gives the Romans their unique power. Their patience, resourcefulness, tenacity, and adaptability are virtues which make a particular appeal to all whose more brilliant interior gifts are cramped by self-consciousness, excessive individualism, and destructive scepticism. The Jews, for all their spiritual greatness, and the Greeks, for all their intellectual power, could never conquer and hold the world as the Romans did, because they were too inflexible or too pliable, too fanatical or too inconsequent, to adjust themselves in practical affairs to varying conditions without surrendering their ulterior purpose. Thus it came about that the Jews handed over to the Roman Empire the task of disseminating the religion they had founded, and the Greeks owed to Roman receptiveness the popularisation of their intellectual discoveries and their artistic inventions.

This Roman genius for *vulgarisation* is despised by extremists, but it was a most valuable gift. To have created a common level of culture over a wide area of the earth, embracing all manner of peoples and beliefs and landscapes, was no commonplace achievement. By making the thought of Greece and Israel generally accessible Rome increased enormously the probability that a few exceptional minds would find their way to the highest things. Without the world-extension of Roman civilisation the Spaniard Hadrian, the Dalmatian Jerome, and the Punic Augustine would presumably have lived and died in obscurity. Thus it is not so much the quality as the quantity of Roman art that ultimately matters. The oecumenical distribution of Roman objects created numberless opportunities for new contacts and the generation of new hybrids. From this point of view the very ordinariness of Roman art becomes a positive virtue.

It is therefore irrelevant to discuss whether the works of art produced round the shores of the Mediterranean during the first four centuries of the Christian era were made by "Greeks" or "Romans". Such racial distinctions are only valid to a very limited extent. It is much more important to discover where an object was made, and for whom, and what beliefs it embodied and was intended to satisfy. Living as we do in an age when art is divorced from life, we are too ready to forget that works of art, like other commodities, can be subject to the laws of supply and demand; and that consequently the consumer as well as the producer can influence their form. The art of the Roman Empire was essentially the result of such co-operation between artist and client; and in the following analysis of its guiding principles three main factors are taken into consideration. The first is the factor of time and space: in what part of the empire was the object produced, and when? These two aspects of production are so closely connected that it is impracticable to treat them separately. The second is the social factor: for whom was the object made—emperor, nobleman, official, soldier, or tradesman? This is a most important matter, yet one which has been strangely neglected. The third factor is functional: what was the purpose of the object—commemorative, symbolic, ornamental, or a mixture of all three in varying proportions? With all these elements to be correlated, it is not surprising that Roman imperial art should sometimes seem baffling and inconclusive. But if it is not easy to manipulate them as dexterously as one could wish, it is at least desirable to know how to recognise them and try to check their mutual reactions.

The first factor—that of date and place—has received the most attention and is therefore the best understood. The main chronological divisions have been fixed with tolerable accuracy, and the regional spheres of influence are being determined with some degree of certainty. It cannot be said, however, that the internal connexion between time and space has been satisfactorily established for all parts of the empire. We know, indeed, that Athens was especially active in the time of Augustus, and again under Hadrian and the early Antonines. The share of Asia Minor, especially in the second century A.D., can also be traced in some detail. But the influence of the two great Hellenistic metropoles, Alexandria and Antioch, remains very obscure, in spite of the large claims that have been made on their behalf and the frequency with which their names and reputations have been brought into the discussion. In the present state of our knowledge it is simpler to pass lightly over these regional distinctions, especially as it can be proved abundantly not only that works of art were habitually exported from one part of the empire to another, but also that the artists themselves migrated freely and that a territorial name in a signature is no guarantee that its owner spent much of his life in his native town. It is more convenient, therefore, to study the evolution of the Roman imperial style as a single continuous process and to note the emergence and eclipse of the various regional creative centres as they occur in time.

In his *Kunstgeschichtliche Grundbegriffe*[1] Wölfflin laid down certain principles of formal development which he applied to the art of the Renascence and Baroque, but which, he suggested, are applicable to other phases of European art. These principles were deduced by observing the internal evolution of the

[1] Translated into English by Hottinger as *Principles of Art History*.

formal sense, which, as he showed, tends to repeat itself automatically in a regular cycle, so long as contingent circumstances are favourable. This process begins with vision itself and the psychological attitude of the artist to the world of sense. It is assumed that he is in full possession of the necessary technical equipment; Wölfflin disregards the "primitive", who has still to overcome primary material obstacles. He begins with artists in the situation of a Greek of the later fifth century B.C., a Roman of the Augustan age, a Frenchman of the mid-thirteenth century, or an Italian about the year 1500. This choice of dates for the beginning of one of Wölfflin's cycles suggests that "classicism" is the starting-point for his theory of form; and this is confirmed by the title of an earlier book, *Klassische Kunst*, in which he studied the art of the High Renascence. As we habitually apply the epithet also to the art of the fifth century B.C., and by extension to other kindred periods, it may be as well to define more exactly what we mean by "classicism", and indicate briefly what classical works of art have in common.

Classicism is popularly supposed to imply maturity; it stands for the middle stage between the tentative experiments of adolescence and the accomplished but retrospective and sterile decline. This metaphor from the stages of human life was discarded by Wölfflin, who was at pains to prove that the change from classic to baroque was not a symptom of degeneration, but merely the transition from one mode of vision to another. He refrained from moral judgements and rejected all aesthetic criticism that regarded baroque as in any way inferior to classic. He simply wished to show that baroque is the inevitable sequel to classic form. After the Parthenon frieze follows the Mausoleum frieze, and after that the Giant frieze of Pergamon; after Rheims, the Chartreuse de Champmol; after Raphael, Michelangelo, and so to Bernini. It remains to be shown that an analogous process takes place in the art of the Roman Empire.

Augustan classicism is a familiar phrase, but Augustan art would more exactly be described as classicist than as classical. The distinction is important. Roman imperial art was born grown-up; it had no childhood and no adolescence, and this abnormal beginning hampered its natural growth for about a century. It started with deliberate imitation, archaism, eclecticism, and other morbid symptoms of a tradition in decline. Only the new content of imperial art saved it from insipidity. The need for historical representations, highly-characterised portraiture, and naturalistic studies of plant-life obliged the late Hellenistic artists of the Augustan age to invent new themes and methods. Motifs from the most various bygone styles were revived, adapted, and synthetically combined; yet in spite of these inconsistencies and the simultaneous practice of several styles, Augustan art can still be called classical in the strictly Wölfflinian sense. It is clear, finite, and static. In an Augustan relief-composition the individual elements are shown in their most evident and apprehensible shape, with sharp outlines, tangible surfaces, and a plain conventional background. There is no mystery; everything is stated unequivocally, and the implication of the whole design is immediately obvious. However near the spectator approaches, the effect remains equally explicit and unmistakable. The relation of the parts to the whole, and of the frame to its contents, is carefully contrived and efficiently presented. Such an art, it is at once understood, belongs entirely to this world. It appeals to the bodily sense of touch. It is rationalistic and humane. Its qualities are intellectual rather than emotional. It expresses to perfection the absolutely secular ambitions of the Roman Empire; and its very virtues imply the dangers which threaten an organisation so exclusively preoccupied with material efficiency.

For there is something airless about the precision of Augustan art which gives it a kind of unreality, for all its manifest qualities. It seems to exist in an ideal vacuum which preserves its contents incorrupt but is unable to sustain life. This is always a weakness to which classical art is liable; and it is through the effort to overcome this defect that the transitional process is observed to begin. In this respect the parallel between the first and the sixteenth centuries is sometimes surprisingly close. In both we watch the precipitation of an atmosphere; the surrounding air is permitted to exercise in art the function that it does in life, veiling slightly the crystalline clarity of the pure form, and introducing a notion of the vague, the relative, and the infinite. At the same time the material substance becomes richer and more complicated. Relief is higher; colour and texture are more intimately and sensuously handled; and the uniformity of the surface is diffracted and dissolved. The artist no longer invites the spectator to touch; he bids him keep his distance and use his eyes.

This impressionist tendency of Flavian art is ascribed now to Asia Minor and now to Alexandria by critics who are unwilling to believe that any artistic process could occur spontaneously in Rome itself, but it is in fact quite unnecessary to look so far afield. The transition from Augustan classicism to Flavian illusionism can be explained more simply as a reversion to the well-known Italic taste for visual rather than tactile effects which has been noticed by students of early Roman portrait-sculpture.[1] It is also relevant to observe that Pompeian painting reached its highest point of development in the Flavian period, when its expansion was interrupted by the disaster of A.D. 79; and that unlike contemporary sculptors, the painters had Latin names—Studius,[2] for example, the Augustan landscapist, and Famullus,[3] the decorator of Nero's Golden House. This pictorial propensity explains why Roman artists took so readily to baroque effects; the substitution of a painterly for a linear conception of form is one of Wölfflin's chief criteria for the substitution of the baroque for the classical style.

No monumental paintings by Flavian artists of the first rank have survived, though the decoration of the latest Pompeian houses, provincial and derivative as it is, allows us to imagine the masterpieces of the capital. The influence of Flavian painting can be inferred, however, in the reliefs on the Arch of Titus.[4]

[1] See Kaschnitz-Weinberg in *RM.*, xli. (1926), pp. 133 ff.
[2] Pliny, *Nat. Hist.*, xxxv. 116.
[3] *Ibid.*, xxxv. 120. Cf. Weege in *JdI.*, xxviii. (1913), pp. 127 ff.
[4] Wickhoff, *Roman Art*, pp. 76 ff.

The contrast between these animated and romantic scenes and the chilly precision of the Ara Pacis is striking still, and must have been even more so when the plastic effect was enhanced by the complementary colouring of the background and accessories which the sculptural treatment presupposes. Wickhoff and others who first perceived the artistic importance of these compositions made somewhat exaggerated claims on their behalf, comparing them with the work of Velazquez and other essentially dissimilar artists; but even if we avoid such far-fetched allusions, we must allow that they are an impressive contribution to baroque relief, and give their designer the credit for solving problems which no Greek sculptor had faced.

The experiment was fruitful. Without the reliefs of the Arch of Titus it would hardly have been possible to invent the noble battlepiece which once adorned the Forum of Trajan and is now built into the central passage of the Arch of Constantine.[1] The tempo is more rapid; the rhythms are contrapuntal. The individual figures overlap and interlace, and their contours emerge and disappear again in the shadowy background, which no longer has any tangible reality, but is just space itself. This relief is historically of great importance, since, dating from the second decade of the century, it anticipates in all essentials the full-blown Antonine baroque of two generations later. The natural development of the imperial style from classic to baroque was

[1] Strong, *Scultura romana*, i. p. 143, and fig. 89; Rodenwaldt, *Kunst der Antike*, p. 574.

momentarily interrupted by an Attic revival under the patronage of the philhellene emperor Hadrian.[1] This is commonly called a classicistic reaction, but such a description is not quite exact. What happened was that Hadrian and the Athenian millionaire Herodes Atticus started a fashion in official circles for the Attic tradition, which had always been in vogue locally, but had recently fallen out of favour in Italy and the eastern provinces. A certain number of public monuments of Hadrianic date are decorated with reliefs which exhibit the usual classical features: sharp outline, crisp modelling, and frieze-composition with all the figures standing on the same level against a plain background. Such, for example, are the medallions with hunting-scenes which now adorn the Arch of Constantine;[2] these look like enlarged coins,[3] and it may be observed that the circular form, which has no functional meaning in this context, is itself used in an unclassical manner.

A good deal of Hadrianic art, however, is not Attic in style and origin. For instance, a relief of Antinous as Silvanus, found at Lanuvium and datable about A.D. 133,[4] is signed by Antonianos of Aphrodisias, a town in Caria which produced a long and successful line of artists, who had the rare and laudable habit of putting their names to their work.[5] This school demonstrates several interesting facts:

[1] Toynbee, *Hadrianic School*, pp. xiii. ff.

[2] Strong, *Scultura romana*, ii. pp. 217 ff. and Figs. 131-8.

[3] For the artistic importance of the Hadrianic coin-issues, cf. Toynbee, *op. cit.*, pp. 24 ff.

[4] Delbrueck, *Antike Porträts*, pl. 44. Brunn-Bruckmann, pl. 635.

[5] Cf. Toynbee, *op. cit.*, pp. xxv; 242 f.

first, that Asia Minor was an important artistic centre in the second century; secondly, that it exported work to various parts of the empire; thirdly, that its members travelled, since the Antinous relief seems to be made of Italian marble, and therefore in Italy; and fourthly, that there is little stylistic continuity between works by various artists of this school—they seem to have been copyists and eclectic artists prepared to work in any of the fashionable styles.

This does not imply, however, that the Asiatic ateliers were unable to formulate a style of their own at this period. The true Asiatic style is seen, not in the decorative and derivative pieces by the artists of Aphrodisias, but in the large baroque sarcophagi which came into fashion about the middle of the century.[1] These are an original invention which exercised a considerable influence on later art and deserve to be studied in some detail. In shape they are rectangular architectural compositions decorated on all four sides with a system of columns, architraves, pediments and niches, which contain small isolated statues in the round. The general scheme goes back to the fourth century B.C., to prototypes like the sarcophagus of the weeping women, found at Sidon and now in the museum at Istanbul;[2] this prototype is itself a reduced version of a Lycian tomb like the Nereid Monument from Xanthos,[3] with its alternating columns and free-standing figures,

[1] Morey, *Sarcophagus of Claudia Antonia Sabina* (*Sardis* v. 1).

[2] Hamdy Bey and Reinach, *Nécropole royale à Sidon*, pls. 4-11. Mendel, *Catalogue*, no. 10.

[3] Niemann, *Das Nereiden-Monument in Xanthos.*

and the persistence of this type of sepulchral edifice can thus be traced in south-western Asia Minor for more than six centuries. The immediate origin of the Antonine sarcophagi, so far as their decoration is concerned, seems, however, to be Athens; some of the early members of the group of Lydian sarcophagi are actually made of Pentelic marble, and the figure-types are distinctly Attic. These sarcophagi were in many cases intended for the western market, and for this reason conform to the Italic scheme by carrying recumbent effigies on the top, instead of the gabled roof which was usual in Asia Minor. This Attic treatment of the figures gave place before long to a more pronouncedly baroque system of decoration based on the ornamental architecture of Asia Minor and Syria. Such compositions as the market-gate of Miletus,[1] the Library at Ephesus,[2] and still more the stage-wall of the theatre at Aspendus[3] and the interior of the great temple at Baalbek,[4] illustrated the picturesque and sumptuous mode of wall-decoration which influenced the design of Asiatic sarcophagi. These purely scenic arrangements of columns and niches seem to be the realisation in three dimensions of the painted stage architecture which we can reconstruct from the frescoes of Pompeii.[5] The structural logic which had regulated the classical building now gives place to non-structural fantasy. Columns and archi-

[1] Now reconstructed in the Berlin museum.

[2] Robertson, *Greek and Roman Architecture*, pp. 289 ff., and figs. 119-20.

[3] *Ibid.*, p. 277 and fig. 117.

[4] *Ibid.*, pp. 228 ff. and pl. 13.

[5] Especially those in the so-called fourth style. For the connexion between these paintings and theatrical scenery, cf. Bulle, *Untersuchungen an griechischen Theatern*, pp. 331, ff.

traves no longer exist to fulfil their primary tectonic purpose; they have become passive from the utilitarian point of view, but actors in a comedy of light and shadow. The modulation of colour and chiaroscuro is now the artist's only care. When architecture is thus converted into a backcloth it is not surprising that the figures also lose their individual importance and act as little more than punctuation-marks in a display of rhetoric. They stand out as patches of white against a black cavern; and as their sole function is to reflect light, they are simplified and flattened and dematerialised as much as possible. The figure and the niche it occupies become a single aesthetic unit; that is why the motif of the *homme-arcade*, as M. Focillon calls it,[1] had so long a life in late antique and early medieval art.

Different in origin, but similar in decorative effect, is the all-over system of composition, the chief rival to the *homme-arcade* in later imperial art. In this the elements of the design are treated individually as units seen in profile, and are then projected on to a vertical surface which stands for the ground seen from a bird's-eye viewpoint. This system has a very long history.[2] It had been used in Assyrian art, but had been rejected by the earlier Greek artists in favour of the frieze-composition which they had learnt from Egypt. When the conquests of Alexander renewed the contact of Greece with the Orient, the eastern panoramic method of composition gradually began to reappear in the Mediterranean world. Its progress was slow at

[1] *L'art des sculpteurs romans*, pp. 67 ff.

[2] Müller in *Archiv für Orientforschung*, v. (1928–9), pp. 199 ff.

first, for the unlimited conception of space which it implied was not congenial to the classical Greek instinct for finite form. But when Roman imperial art had shaken itself free from Greek formal prejudices, the panoramic method was found to satisfy the Roman desire for wide spaces, multitudinous activity, and the continuous representation of successive events in a single scene.[1] The first experiments with this method of composition can be found in Roman wall-paintings of the first century of the empire;[2] and it is clear that such a method is particularly appropriate to the art of painting, which deals specifically with an ideal space. But in the next century it appears extended to the art of sculpture in the helical relief-band of the Column of Trajan.

The Column of Trajan is the characteristic monument of the age and perhaps the most remarkable single achievement of Roman art.[3] In it the imperial spirit finds full expression for the first time; and as the spirit is new, so is the form which embodies it. Trajan was the first of the provincial emperors, a Spaniard from Andalusia; and his memorial is the first masterpiece of the art of the whole empire. It is neither Greek nor Italian, but Roman.[4] In style it is curiously unofficial. The court-tradition of the Ara Pacis, the Arch of Titus, and even Trajan's own arch at Benevento, has no place here. It is a work

[1] Cf. Wickhoff, *Roman Art*, pp. 8 ff., 163 ff.

[2] E.g. in the Odyssey landscapes in the Vatican Library: Nogara, *Nozze aldobrandine*, pls. 9 ff.

[3] Lehmann-Hartleben, *Die Trajanssäule*.

[4] Cf. Ferri, *L'arte romana sul Reno*, pp. 260 ff.

of popular art. To a Greek, a column on this scale, architectonic in form but not in function, and surrounded by a continuous helical band of reliefs would have seemed a monstrosity; it is interesting to guess what Apollodorus of Damascus, the architect of the Forum that contained it, thought of this audacious contrivance. This is provincial taste, he must have said to himself. But something new and profoundly significant had happened. A new race had suddenly found a shape for its own self-consciousness.

This brings us to the social factor; and we have to consider how the style of Roman imperial art was affected by the varying rank and aspirations of the men who commissioned it. Most of the monuments we have examined so far were ordered by the state or by rich private individuals; and in these some form of Hellenic taste predominates, at least in externals. But the Column of Trajan, as we have just noted, shows the emergence of a new formal sense, in which Hellenic preconceptions play a comparatively small part.[1] Efforts have been made to find a prototype for the Trajanic monument on the Rhine, and notably in the column dedicated to Nero (A.D. 66) at Mainz;[2] this is decorated with superposed zones of relief, not with a continuous helical band, but the fundamental principle is the same. What is perhaps more significant, however, is that in the handling of the figures, and in their relation to the landscape they occupy, the reliefs of the Column of Trajan anticipate the composition of many late-antique and early

[1] Cf. Ferri, *op. cit.*, pp. 211 ff.

[2] Strong, *Scultura romana*, i. pp. 98 ff. and figs. 68–9.

Plate II medieval scenes.[1] The bird's-eye viewpoint, the disproportion between the figures and the architectural accessories, the narrative vivacity, and a certain naivety in the treatment of the individual forms have suggested to recent students that there must have existed in Rome, alongside of the court ateliers with their Hellenic traditions, provincial ateliers which worked in quite a different style.[2] These were mainly occupied with commissions for funerary monuments from modest and obscure personages, and only now emerge into the public world of state undertakings and imperial propaganda. This theory is supported by the existence of works like the Monument of the Haterii,[3] the remains of which are now in the Lateran Museum; its reliefs are totally un-Greek in their imaginative and illogical method of conceiving space, and their kinship with later compositions is evident to anyone who studies them with this relation in mind.

From these examples we may therefore deduce that the late antique style in the west is not so much a natural development of Graeco-Roman form as the triumph in official circles of a tradition which had been created by the artisan class and propagated from one part of the empire to another by the army and by traders. These movements of popular taste were greatly reinforced by the spread of various new religions, mainly of oriental origin, in the later Roman Empire; and this fact obliges us to reckon

[1] Cf. Lehmann-Hartleben, *op. cit.*, p. 153 f.
[2] Ferri, *op. cit.*, pp. 231 ff.
[3] Strong, *op. cit.*, i. p. 130 f., and fig. 83.

II. DETAIL FROM THE COLUMN OF TRAJAN
Rome, Foro Traiano.

with the third factor mentioned above—namely, the functional factor. What was the purpose of the object we are considering? Was it commemorative, symbolic, or just ornamental? Nearly always, we find, it was a mixture of all three, but the emphasis on one or another function has a considerable effect on the form.

Official Roman art is primarily commemorative, like that of ancient Egypt or Mesopotamia, but unlike that of Periclean Athens. If we compare the frieze of the Parthenon with that of the Ara Pacis the distinction between Greek and Roman methods becomes immediately obvious. In the Parthenon the triumph of the Athenian Empire is represented symbolically by the Panathenaic procession.[1] In the Ara Pacis[2] the triumph of Augustus is explicitly indicated by a group-portrait of the imperial family, men and women, old and young, wending its way to the sacrifice. The atmosphere is entirely different; in the former, the secular event is transposed on to an ideal plane and visualised by the symbolic eye of the imagination, whereas in the latter a real moment of history is fixed in artistic shape. This distinction persists throughout the empire and lives on into the Middle Ages. Symbolical figures and groups retain their Greek form with a remarkable tenacity; and even when the abstraction symbolised changes its meaning, the symbol remains the same. It is unnecessary to repeat for the hundredth time that pagan

[1] For an aesthetic analysis of the frieze, see von Lücken, *Parthenonskulpturen*, pp. 13 ff.

[2] Strong, *Scultura romana*, i. pp. 28 ff., figs. 17-21.

cupids become Christian cherubs, and victories angels. The important point is that these types are of Greek invention, not Roman or eastern; the Greek contribution to medieval iconography is to be found especially in the apocalyptic scenes. It was the Romans who gave the decisive impulse to the formation of the Christian legend in its pictorial shape, because it was they who created the historical-narrative conception of a scene in its European form.

The Roman contribution to the ornamental art of the Mediterranean world has been misjudged and misinterpreted; and if we are to understand the principles of medieval decoration, we must first decide how Roman ornament differed from the Greek. Again we find the antithesis between symbolism and naturalism which distinguishes the Greek from the Roman attitude to a historical event. The Greek treatment of a decorative element like a lotus-bud or an acanthus-scroll is intellectual, not sensuous.[1] The structural facts of nature are studied and respected but they are not imitated literally. The Greek artist observes how the plant is articulated, and then he invents an organism which is articulated in the same way; the derivative resembles its prototype by analogy, not by identity. The Roman decorative artist, on the other hand, starts with a visual impression and works perceptually, not conceptually. Again we observe the transition, according to the Wölfflinian scheme, from the linear to the painterly approach to form, from classical intellectuality to

[1] Cf. Jacobsthal, *Ornamente griechischer Vasen*, pp. 81 ff.

baroque sensuousness. Even in the classicising phases of Roman taste the attitude to ornament is fundamentally unclassical. Attic palmettes and acanthus-leaves occur in their classical shape on monuments explicitly modelled on originals of the fifth century B.C., but such archaising work is not really significant. For the true Roman conception of decorative art we must go to the painted flower-beds in the Villa of Livia at Prima Porta.[1] Here the walls of a small room are covered all over with a garden-scene from floor to ceiling; the painted surface is continuous, without any architectural frame or subdivisions—merely an inconspicuous cornice and leafy pelmet, and the tangible reality of the wall is denied. There are no known Hellenistic examples of such a vista-composition; and it is doubtful whether Greek taste would have endured a wall-decoration in which the physical existence of the wall was so completely ignored, and from which all traces of human life were excluded. We have to go back to Minoan times in order to find a mural composition on this scale in which man has no place.[2]

At Prima Porta the Roman passion for topiary landscape is exhibited in its extreme form; but it is easy to find evidence for a love of plants, fruit, and flowers in Roman decorative art in which a scientific interest in specific form and an aesthetic sense of beautiful shape are simultaneously expressed. Wreaths as an artistic fashion were invented in the fourth

[1] Retouched chromolithograph in *Antike Denkmäler*, i. (1886), pl. 11; reproduction from photograph in Rizzo, *Pittura ellenistico-romana*, pls. 181–2.

[2] Forsdyke, *Minoan Art* (*Proceedings of the British Academy*, xv.).

century B.C.;[1] and garlands and other flower motifs are comparatively common in Hellenistic art. But if we compare the swags on a Hellenistic altar like that in the precinct of the theatre of Dionysus at Athens[2] with those from the Ara Pacis,[3] we find that the Greek fruit and leaves are conventional and abstract, whereas the Roman are studied leaf by leaf and fruit by fruit, each being differentiated and given an individual value, without, however, impairing the decorative unity of the whole. Like all the sculpture on the Ara Pacis this swag has the sharpness and finiteness of a classical conception in any medium. The inevitable transition to baroque illusionism is seen on the relief in the Lateran,[4] of Flavian date, which shows an ornamental column entwined with sprays of wild rose. The lucid statement of the Ara Pacis relief is replaced by hints at movement, by a certain atmospheric vagueness, and by an unsubstantial poise of the column in space; it has no weight, but hovers in mid-air, permitting the rose-tendrils to wind even under its base. This volatilisation of the material world is a well-known phenomenon of baroque art; and, as we shall see in the next chapter, it was a valuable accessory experience when late-antique artists had to cope with the problems of transcendental expression.

It will be convenient to summarise in a few words this threefold analysis of Roman imperial art from

[1] Pliny, *Nat. Hist.*, xxxv. 125. Cf. Pfuhl, *Malerei und Zeichnung der Griechen*, ii. pp. 731 ff.

[2] Rodenwaldt, *Kunst der Antike*, p. 482.

[3] *Ibid.*, p. 519.

[4] Wickhoff, *Roman Art*, pl. 8, opp. p. 56.

the respective standpoints of date and place, of social requirements, and of functional content. We have seen that the Hellenistic centres of Athens, Asia Minor, Antioch, and Alexandria continue in the Roman world to exert their old creative influence and to preserve the continuity of technical tradition in a changing society. We have also seen that the political rise of Italy, and later of the western provinces, profoundly modified the Hellenistic formal idiom by making new demands which were partly material, but chiefly psychological. The cultivated cosmopolitan taste of Athens and Alexandria had to be at once simplified and intensified to suit the lower, but wider, level of culture in the New World of the western Mediterranean. The modern parallel of the mutual reactions of European and American civilisation will occur to everybody. We have noted, moreover, that the change from a symbolical to a commemorative conception of art, and from an intellectual to a sensuous attitude to form, involves technical changes from the classical to the baroque manner which are to some extent inherent in the evolution of every artistic style, but which were particularly favoured by the circumstances of Roman imperial civilisation.

II

THE civilisation of the Roman world was essentially secular;[1] it took for granted that power and success, order and prosperity were the highest ambitions of man. The worship of the old gods survived, but less from a conviction of its spiritual value than because of the opportunity it provided for ceremonial and pageantry. Many new cults also appeared and found favour; but their social importance was indirect, since they catered for the needs of the separate individual, not for the corporate desire of the whole community. The real goddess whom all united to adore was Fortuna. While the empire was expanding, the consequences of this materialistic outlook were a high level of comfort and amenity for the privileged classes and an outward appearance of great civic splendour, for the Romans had inherited the Greek conception of the successful man's duty to his native town and it had become the fashion for every wealthy citizen to compete with his neighbours in endowing magnificent works of public utility. But this lavish expenditure was ultimately unproductive because it expressed no higher aim than communal self-indulgence, and because it was more or less consciously intended as an opiate for the unrest of the slave-masses. *Panem et circenses* has become the proverbial care of a

[1] See Rostovtsev, *Social and Economic History of the Roman Empire*, pp. viii. ff. and *passim*.

government which denies its subjects any share in the management of their country; and this famous phrase conveniently sums up the materialistic shortcomings of Roman civilisation.

While the empire was expanding, the defects of the system remained latent;[1] but under Trajan this expansion came to an end. Hadrian aimed at consolidating and stabilising the empire within the territorial limits then reached. He attempted to create a sense of Mediterranean nationality, in which differences of race and status and culture were to be adjusted to an equal level. We have already mentioned the advantages of this *Gleichschaltung*, which had so much in common with the liberal internationalism of the nineteenth century. But like its successor, it was premature and impracticable. The so-called "Golden Age" of the Antonines is now seen to have suffered from the weaknesses to which other gold standards are prone; it was artificial, precarious, and inelastic. The privilege of material prosperity was dearly bought, not so much in money as in the sacrifice of moral and spiritual qualities. This interior emptiness of Roman civilisation is strikingly analysed in one of Gregory the Great's sermons: "There was long life and health, material prosperity, growth of population and the tranquillity of daily peace, yet while the world was still flourishing in itself, in their hearts it had already withered."[2] It is no accident that the most intelligent of the Antonine emperors should have

[1] See Christopher Dawson's Essay, "The Dying World", in *A Monument to St. Augustine*, pp. 15 ff.

[2] Homilies xxviii. (Migne lxxvi. col. 1212), quoted by Dawson, *op. cit.*, p. 25.

been the most melancholy and disillusioned, and the most unfortunate in his successor, the son whom he had so carefully educated to face his crushing responsibilities, and who so wantonly evaded them.[1]

The best evidence for the change of spiritual atmosphere during the course of the second century may be found by comparing the reliefs of the Column of Trajan with those of its imitator, the column set up by the Senate and the Roman people to commemorate the campaigns of Marcus Aurelius against the Marcomanni in 169–72 and the Sarmatians in 174–6.[2] It is a fortunate thing for the student of Roman art that the two chief masterpieces of this decisive century of its development should be so explicitly related to each other; in most cases the comparison of works of art is a comparison of incommensurables, but here the avowed dependence of the Aurelian upon the Trajanic column permits us to distinguish accurately between their aims and methods. For the resemblance, though obvious, is superficial. The general plan of the Trajanic column, with its helical band bearing representations of the two Dacian campaigns separated by a victory writing upon a shield, is repeated upon the Aurelian column; but the difference in the manner of envisaging the scenes and treating the individual episodes is so pronounced that it would hardly be an exaggeration, from some points of view, to place the dividing line between ancient and medieval art in

[1] Cf. Renan, *Marc-Aurèle*, pp. 464 ff.

[2] Calderini, Domaszewski, and Petersen, *Die Marcus-Säule*; see also Wegner in *JdI.* xlvi. (1931), pp. 61 ff.

the seventy or eighty years that separate the two monuments.

We have already noted that the relation of figures to landscape in the reliefs of Trajan's column foreshadows the methods of late-antique and early medieval art. This resemblance is chiefly technical; the use of the continuous style, the panoramic treatment of space, the conventional treatment of the architecture and other accessories afford many parallels with the idioms of a later period. But in other respects the art of the Trajanic column is essentially antique in spirit. The attitude of the artist to his theme is objective; he is concerned with historical narrative, and his first anxiety is to represent the actual episodes of war as plausibly as possible. To be sure, he allows himself a certain poetic licence; the appearance and reappearance of the emperor in person at crucial moments occur with such dramatic aplomb that we are aware of a certain legitimate artifice in the management of the story. The narrator makes no comment, however, upon the spiritual significance of the events he describes. The necessity for the war is taken for granted; the moral justification of Roman policy is felt to require no apology; and if any compassion is felt for the defeat of a brave enemy—and the scene of the Dacian chiefs taking poison within the walls of Sarmizegetusa[1] suggests such a natural emotion—these human asides are comparatively rare and are never underlined. This extreme restraint is stoical in the antique Roman fashion; it is not at all inconsistent with the hard, undeviating tenour of the whole

[1] Lehmann-Hartleben, pl. 48, sec. ciii.

conception. The Dacians are beaten because they are barbarians; no other outcome of a Roman campaign could possibly be contemplated.

The atmosphere of the Aurelian column is utterly different. The magnificent complacency of the Trajanic monument has evaporated. The Romans no longer triumph by right, as a result of their own superior exertion; in a crisis they are saved by a miracle, the storm of rain which overwhelms the Sarmatians, while refreshing the drought-stricken Romans.[1] We are inevitably reminded of the crossing of the Red Sea; and the introduction of this supernatural incident marks a decisive stage in the dematerialisation of art which characterises the late-antique, as opposed to the classical, attitude to the world. It is remarkable, moreover, how the scenic conception of the space in which the action takes place is now modified to suit the more mythical conception of the event. The precisely detailed, if somewhat naively imagined, landscape of the Trajanic column is greatly simplified and rarefied in its later counterpart. Trees and rocks and buildings no longer have any independent existence. If they are not necessary for the narrative, they are omitted. The space becomes abstract and shadowy; the ground on which the figures stand consists of mere ledges shelved out from the ideal backcloth, as on the somewhat earlier *decursio*-scene on the base of the column of Antoninus Pius now in the Giardino della Pigna at the Vatican.[2] On the other hand, the flat tapestried effect of the

[1] Petersen, *op. cit.*, p. 58 f.
[2] Strong, *Scultura romana*, ii. p. 248, fig. 152.

Trajanic reliefs is replaced by new suggestions of depth and atmosphere. The actual undercutting of the relief is considerably deeper on the Aurelian than on the Trajanic column; and instead of being applied like separate and detachable units to a uniform background, the individual figures and groups are now sandwiched into each other and overlapped in a much more baroque manner. At the same time, the continuous flow of the Trajanic relief is broken up into smaller and more easily isolated groups; and there is a noticeable tendency, in the scenes where the emperor is shown haranguing his men, to present the imperial party as a centralised and frontalised nucleus, and to arrange the audience in a ring all round. The significance of this scheme, as anticipating early medieval design, has been recently discussed by Wegner, whose illuminating comparisons we shall consider subsequently.[1]

These technical devices for the realisation of a spatial sense at once more concentrated and also more abstract than its classical predecessor are matched by a new attitude to the individual figures and their spiritual relationships. The emotional tension is higher. Especially in the battle-scenes there is a more deliberate emphasis on the horrors of war; something of the relish of pacifist propaganda appears in the scenes of mutilation and torture; and the prisoners themselves invariably wear a wild and tragic aspect which seems hysterical compared with the behaviour of the Dacians on the Column of Trajan.

The expressionist and baroque tendencies exhibited

[1] Below, pp. 128, 135.

in the design of the Aurelian column appear in an intensified form in certain reliefs of the Severan period such as the enormous and elaborate sarcophagus from the Villa Ludovisi now in the Museo Nazionale in Rome.[1] This masterpiece of late Roman relief is of great technical and aesthetic interest. The composition of the battlepiece which covers the entire front is colouristic, not plastic. Unity is achieved by the distribution of light and shadow so as to create an evenly modulated texture rather than a precise linear pattern. The surface-variety, which forms, as it were, a *stretto* in this visual counterpoint,[2] is provided by the tightening of the rhythm in the hair and beards of the barbarians, the horses' manes, the fringes of the Roman soldiers' tunics, and the chain-mail of the trophy-bearer on the extreme right. The congestion of the figures, the elimination of the background, the suppression of space by crowding all the elements into the foreground-plane illustrate the essential principles of baroque design in its most acute form; no single figure is seen in its entirety, the outlines pursue each other among the shadows, and instead of a neutral plane, which by a simple convention we understand as air, the actual air of a dark cave fills the narrow interstices between the solid bodies of the foreground.

The extreme physical complexity of the composi-

[1] Rodenwaldt, *Kunst der Antike*, pp. 616-21. Strong, *op. cit.*, ii. p. 327, fig. 200.

[2] This metaphor from music is not arbitrary and irrelevant; polyphony was invented in northern Europe, and its baroque complexity is the auditual counterpart of late Gothic visual form: see Schlosser, *Präludien*, pp. 205 ff.

III. DETAIL FROM THE LUDOVISI BATTLE-SARCOPHAGUS: DYING BARBARIAN
Rome, Museo Nazionale.

tion matches the violent emotion displayed by the individual figures, and especially by the dying barbarians who are being mown down by the Roman soldiery. One of these heads is here reproduced in detail;[1] detached from its context, it has an extraordinary resemblance to a late Gothic Christ in Agony, or even a seventeenth-century version of the same theme. It almost tempts us to trace some Teutonic neurosis in this recurrent theme, for the barbarian seems to be of Nordic race; is it possible that the designer of this remarkable relief, so full of Gothic unrest and exaltation, was himself of German stock—a spiritual ancestor of Grünewald?

Plate III opp. p. 30

The connexion between this almost pathological emotion and the density of the plastic arrangement is perhaps not entirely accidental; parallel phenomena may be found in the Scythian animal-style,[2] in certain Carolingian ivories to be discussed below, in fifteenth-century South German altarpieces,[3] in various pictures by El Greco,[4] and in certain contemporary expressionist and surrealist paintings.[5] Whether or not there is a real psychological relation between an art which is only obliquely concerned with the objective world and this insensibility to

[1] Rodenwaldt, *Kunst der Antike*, p. 621. I am indebted to the kindness of Prof. Rodenwaldt for permission to publish this photograph by Frau Rodenwaldt.

[2] Borovka, *Scythian Art*, pl. 51.

[3] See e.g. the high altar by Michael Pacher at St. Wolfgang: Sauerlandt, *Deutsche Plastik des Mittelalters*, pl. 100.

[4] E.g. the *Resurrection* in the Prado: Cassou, *El Greco*, pl. 12.

[5] See Neumeyer in *Zeitschr. f. bild. Kunst*, lxi. (1927–8), p. 71: "je spiritualistischer ein Stil, desto weniger herrscht die normale, vom Gegenstand her diktierte Distanz."

spatial values, it is certainly noticeable that the artist who is most concerned with spiritual truths often expresses them not by adopting the calligraphic idiom of Chinese art, which attained to transcendent reality by a process of disembodiment, but rather by insisting with an almost obsessive vehemence upon the solidity of material substances. M. Cassou has well described this achievement of supra-real effects by super-objectivity in his analysis of the poetic style of Góngora compared with the pictorial style of El Greco: "Tout est objet: objet dense, épais, volumineux et magnifique, mais objet et rien qu' objet . . . tout est pressé et inséparable, livide et plombé, tout est dur. Aucun joint par où respirer. L'espace a disparu, l'air est absent. Rien ne vibre. Le ciel lui-même est une chose, une chose de carton ou de métal."[1]

The modes of suggesting psychological tension employed by the expressionists of the third century were not invented by them. They had been introduced by Scopas the sculptor[2] and, it seems, by the elder Aristides the painter[3] as long ago as the fourth century B.C.; but in Hellenistic and early imperial art they were mainly used for mythological types such as satyrs, for the representation of slaves and barbarians, and occasionally for the rendering of heroes in exceptionally distracting situations—Niobe or Laocoon, for instance. In portraiture they were inconsistent with the Greek conception of ideal form

[1] Cassou, *El Greco*, p. 43 f.

[2] Richter, *Sculpture and Sculptors of the Greeks*², p. 81.

[3] Pfuhl, *Malerei und Zeichnung der Griechen*, ii. pp. 746 ff.

and with Roman *gravitas*. But this notion that educated people do not betray their emotions was a prejudice of the upper class. It had never existed in the lower ranks of society; and in so far as these could afford to be commemorated in public monuments, their features are found to be more vividly particularised than those of their social superiors. This expressive vernacular style may be seen in innumerable Italic terracotta votive heads,[1] in the ancestral masks of the Republican period,[2] and in the modest tomb-reliefs made under the empire;[3] it is also well represented in the provincial art of the Rhine and the Danube.[4] The heads on various reliefs from Neumagen on the Moselle, now at Trier,[5] are particularly interesting to the student of portraiture, since they show a love of the picturesque and the dramatic that seems entirely disinterested; there is no reason, from the external point of view, why these bearded old Germans should beam or glare as they do, and this determination to be expressive at all costs strikes us as significant when we call to mind the later history of Germanic art.

In the third century this cult of expression makes its appearance in the official portraiture of the capital. The bust of the emperor Philip the Arabian,[6] now in the Vatican, is full of repressed anger; and in

[1] Cf. Kaschnitz-Weinberg in *RM.*, xli. (1926), pp. 133 ff.

[2] Zadoks-Jitta, *Ancestral Portraiture in Rome.*

[3] Altmann, *Römische Grabaltäre der Kaiserzeit.*

[4] Ferri, *Arte romana sul Reno. id.*, *Arte romana sul Danubio.*

[5] Massow, *Grabmäler von Neumagen*, no. 287, pls. 54-5. Details in Rodenwaldt, *Kunst der Antike*, pp. 624-7.

[6] Hekler, *Greek and Roman Portraits*, pl. 293.

Copenhagen there is a wonderful study of an introspective woman of the same period (*c.* A.D. 250).[1] This remarkable outbreak of realism, just at the point when European art was about to forsake realism for centuries to come, can be explained in various ways.[2] It was partly due to a revival of the Italic genius, which had prospered under the Flavians but lost favour under the Atticising Hadrian and at the Syrian court of the later Antonines; the proletarian tendency of the age,[3] when the imperial throne was more than once occupied by some sergeant-major from beyond the pale, probably had a good deal to do with this contempt for the elegant party-manners of Antonine portraiture; and the prevailing uncertainty would be quite sufficient in itself to explain the furrowed brows, the wrinkled cheeks, and strained eyes that we encounter in so many third-century heads. It is interesting to note, however, that a contemporary philosopher observes the movement in taste and defends it on ethical grounds. "Why", inquires Plotinus, "are the most living portraits the most beautiful, even if the others happen to be more symmetric? Why is the living ugly more attractive than the sculptured handsome? It is because the one is more nearly what we are looking for, and this because there is soul there, because there is more of the idea of the Good, because there is some glow of the light of the Good, and this illumination awakens and lifts the soul and all that goes with it, so that the whole

[1] Hekler, *Greek and Roman Portraits*, pl. 303.

[2] See L'orange, *Studien zur Geschichte des spätantiken Porträts*, pp. 1 ff.

[3] Cf. Rostovtsev, *Social and Economic History of the Roman Empire*, pp. 479 ff.

man is won over to goodness and in the fullest measure stirred to life."[1] This curious argument, so difficult to follow in itself, both explains and is explained by the transition from the accomplished realism of the middle of the century to the deliberately unnaturalistic style of its close. The modern analogy of the evolution of nineteenth-century art from the standpoint of Manet to that of Van Gogh[2] may help us to understand what happened to Roman portrait-sculpture in the last decades of the third century; but the passage of Plotinus just quoted provides the philosophic justification. "It is because there is soul there." The brilliant characterisation of the Philippus Arabs is not the antithesis of Constantinian stylisation, as the older critics used to maintain; on the contrary, realism is the necessary preparation for the supra-realism, or magic realism, of late antique art.[3] This discovery of the soul was of incalculable importance for the development of Christian art. Platonism had introduced the spiritual life into the art of the Hellenistic age; and now Neoplatonism reinterpreted that spirit in a more specifically supernatural sense.

This new transcendental quality makes its first appearance in portraiture, and not in narrative art, because only the portrait-tradition at this period was at once sufficiently highly developed to admit so delicate a responsibility and sufficiently vital to endure the necessary change. It was some while before

[1] *Enneades*, vi. 7. 22 (trans. MacKenna and Page, vol. v. p. 189 f.).
[2] Cf. du Colombier and Manuel, *Tableau du XX. siècle: Les arts*, p. 123 f.
[3] Cf. Kaschnitz-Weinberg in *Die Antike*, ii. (1926), pp. 36 ff.

an explicitly Christian narrative art could be brought into existence; the old tradition of the Trajanic and Aurelian columns had dwindled into something essentially poor and even barbarous during the third century, as we can see by comparing the historical reliefs on the Arches of Septimius Severus[1] and Constantine,[2] which mark respectively the beginning and end of that period. Not until the fifth century do we find the first traces of a monumental Christian art in which the form is worthy of the content; during the first century of the peace of the Church, the age of the Fathers and the great Councils, the dignity of Christian imagery is sustained by the imperial effigy. It is the enthroned emperor and empress who provide the types for the enthroned Christ and the Mother of God.[3]

It must be remembered that these imperial effigies are not simply the likenesses of individual men and women. They are something less and something more. If we look in vain for a human counterpart of the Philippus Arabs, we are rewarded by a vision of more than earthly dignity and splendour. The new totalitarian state which Diocletian built upon the ruins of the old empire was presided over by a ruler more than half divine. The colossal heads of Constantine or Constantius II are no ordinary portraits of

[1] Strong, *Scultura romana*, ii. pp. 303 ff. and pls. 60–2.

[2] *Ibid.*, pp. 331 ff., pls. 67–8, and figs. 201–8; cf. Riegl, *Spätrömische Kunstindustrie*[2], pp. 85 ff., where a gallant, but only partly convincing, attempt is made to prove that the deformations of this official-popular art are deliberate.

[3] The headless porphyry statue at Alexandria sometimes described as a Pantocrator is more probably an imperial portrait: see Delbrueck, *Antike Porphyrwerke*, pp. 96 ff., pls. 40–41 (Diocletian?).

ordinary men.[1] They have the remoteness, the intensity, the immutability of cult-images; and only a minor change is necessary to convert them into the Byzantine Pantokrator, and to model a hierarchy of saints upon the personnel of the imperial court.

This hieratic tradition is derived, like other aspects of the Diocletianic state, from Sasanian Persia. It is expressed by pictorial rather than plastic means, since it is more convenient to suggest the mystic nature of the supernatural world by means of the ideal space created by paint—and still better, by mosaic—than with the too solid and earthbound shapes of stone. It is this need for a transcendental world that explains why the only Byzantine sculpture in the round is to be seen in imperial portraits; and why in the fictitious space of the painter's imagination the concrete realities of this life are subtilised and extenuated by a hundred skilful devices.

The technique by which this transcendental world was made just sufficiently accessible to earthly understanding had long been practised in the east. The discovery of some frescoes at Dura-Europos[2] on the Euphrates shows that all the essential features of the hieratic style existed in Mesopotamia at least as far back as the end of the first and the beginning of the second centuries, and probably much earlier; in these processional compositions from the Temple of the Palmyrene Gods we encounter the frontal arrange-

[1] Delbrueck, *Spätantike Kaiserporträts*, pls. 37-9, 52-4.

[2] Breasted, *Oriental Forerunners of Byzantine Painting*, pls. viii. ff.; Cumont, *Fouilles de Doura-Europos*, pp. 41 ff.

ment of the figures in a stiff row, the hovering pose with the feet dangling just above the ground instead of standing firmly on it, and the linear technique which emphasises the contours of the figure at the expense of the surface-modelling in light and shade.

The background of the Dura frescoes is a simple wall with occasional subdivision by pilasters, which tend to occur between the figures, thus producing the *homme-arcade* which we have already noted on the Asiatic sarcophagi of the Lycian type. This adjustment of the figure to an architectural setting appears in a more elaborate shape at the beginning of the fifth century in the cupola-mosaics of the church of St. George at Salonica.[1] Here everything points to contact with the east: in the first place, the choice of saints, who all belong to the oriental calendar and date from before the peace of the Church; secondly, the Syrian elements in the fantastic architecture[2] which is thought to derive from the scenery of the Antiochene theatre; and thirdly, the gold ground, on which the architecture is silhouetted.

The use of a gold background is undoubtedly an oriental device which is more or less consciously intended to break up the illusionistic conception of the picture-space.[3] The glittering surface, which changes in brightness with the smallest movement on

[1] Kömstedt, *Vormittelalterliche Malerei*, fig. 54.

[2] For the disembodiment of the figures, and their fluid relations with the architectural setting, cf. the silver disk of Theodosius in Madrid, which was also probably made at Salonica in 388: Delbrueck, *Consular-Diptychen*, no. 63.

[3] Cf. Paulus Silentiarius, 489 ff., 668 ff. on the gold mosaics in the dome of S. Sophia; see Friedländer, p. 287 f.

IV. IVORY DIPTYCH: THE POET AND HIS MUSE
Monza, Cathedral Treasury.

the spectator's part and the slightest alteration in the natural lighting, effectively destroys all visual associations with this world; it creates a celestial envelope of light, in which bodies lose their corporeality and float and hover exempt from the laws of terrestrial gravity. The gold ground is thus peculiarly favourable to the transcendental atmosphere which the hieratic style exists to convey.

This radiant setting is probably borrowed from the Mazdaean, or perhaps the Manichaean,[1] art of Iran. To the same source Diez has ingeniously ascribed the levitating pose of the figures which inhabit the universe of light;[2] and other characteristics of the hieratic style alluded to above—arrangement of figures in frontal ranks, stylised uniformity of gesture, definition of form by linear instead of plastic means —may equally well descend from Persian prototypes. Whatever their origin, however, these features certainly become increasingly pronounced in the mosaics of the later fifth and sixth centuries. If we compare the circular frieze of Apostles in the dome of the Orthodox Baptistery at Ravenna[3] (*c.* 449–58) with the similar ring in the Baptistery of the Arians[4] (*c.* 500), the stiffening, isolating, and dematerialising process has sensibly advanced. In the ritual processions of male and female saints down the nave of S. Apollinare Nuovo,[5] which date from after the middle of

[1] Cf. Arnold, *Survivals of Sasanian and Manichean Art in Persian Painting.*

[2] *Byzantine Mosaics in Greece*, p. 29.

[3] Kömstedt, *Vormittelalterliche Malerei*, fig. 57.

[4] *Ibid.*, fig. 58.

[5] *Ibid.*, figs. 62–3.

the sixth century, we perceive the value of that simultaneous repetition of gesture which has always been appreciated by choreographers, sacred or profane.

These examples have been chosen from Ravenna, where the western tradition of plastic illusionism survived in detail despite the advances of an alien method of design, because it is no longer possible to find examples of the hieratic style on a monumental scale in Syria and Egypt, countries which were geographically nearer to its source. But certain pieces of minor art,[1] such as textiles and carved ivories, allow us to imagine what these lost masterpieces may have looked like; and as it was these, and not their monumental counterparts, that transmitted the late-antique hieratic tradition to medieval Europe, they thus acquire an importance out of proportion to their intrinsic merit. And since, in the absence of other material, almost all the Carolingian sculpture discussed below will be chosen perforce from ivory-carvings, it will be convenient to describe here some of the fifth- and sixth-century prototypes on which they were modelled.

In examining the late-antique ivories produced in the eastern half of the Roman Empire, we are again struck by the importance of the *homme-arcade* motif. In at least one instance, the diptych in the cathedral-treasury at Monza[2] with a poet and his muse on the two leaves, the actual figures are derived from the

Plate IV opp. p. 38

[1] For a general view of early Byzantine applied art see Peirce and Tyler, *L'art byzantin*, vols. i. and ii.

[2] Weitzmann and Schultz in *JdI.*, xlix. (1934), pp. 128 ff. identify the poet as Claudian and date the diptych *c.* 400.

sarcophagus-repertory, for just these types occur on a fragmentary relief now in the British Museum.[1] This motif is significant, moreover, since it provided, as Friend has shown,[2] the familiar type of the Evangelist composing his Gospel which occurs in the Carolingian MSS. of the Ada School and their many descendants. In this connexion the Monza diptych is of great interest, as the architectural framework is designed in a sort of perspective which seems to have attracted the Carolingian copyist not a little; it frequently appears—misunderstood, it may be, and distorted, but unmistakable—both in book-paintings and ivory-carvings. In the Monza panels not only are the individual figures inspired by classical types, but they are also placed in a more or less coherent tract of space. This structural logic no longer obtains in the well-known panel with the Archangel Michael in the British Museum.[3] At first sight the figure seems to obey the canons of classical sculpture. The features have the regular rounded beauty of the antique type; the drapery is plastically designed, and its folds comply with the conventions of ancient dress; the detail is carefully, even exquisitely, rendered; and the general execution is highly conscientious and accomplished. The architectural frame is likewise entirely plausible, and may be paralleled in actual constructions of the fifth century, such as the Syrian churches of Rusapha and Kalat Seman. But when we examine the relation of the figure to its

Plate V opp. p. 42

[1] *Cat. of Sculpture*, no. 2312.
[2] *Art Studies*, v. (1927), pp. 143 ff.
[3] Dalton, *Cat. of Ivories*, no. 11, pp. 9 ff., pl. 6.

setting, we realise that the illusionist conception of space has broken down. We first observe that the feet, instead of resting on one of the six steps, skim over three of them without touching any; and then we note that though the feet seem at least to be near, if not actually touching, the top steps at the back of the niche, nevertheless the Archangel's arms, and even his right wing, are in quite a different plane, much nearer the spectator. We are thus forced to conclude that if the spatial consistency of the design is to survive, we must interpret the feet as in no way connected with the steps, but hovering in mid-air between the bases of the columns; thus the Archangel becomes another of those levitating figures inspired by Mazdaean ideas, and not the classical being we had at first recognised. Slight as it seems, this point is actually of some consequence,[1] because contemporary figures of earthly personages, like the Monza Muse and Poet or the portraits of the Empress Ariadne in Vienna and Florence (*c.* 480),[2] are still rooted to the ground in the ordinary way.

In spite of these spatial ambiguities the British Museum Archangel is, from the Wölfflinian point of view, classically composed. Although the relief is fairly high in places, the contours of the figure are everywhere sharply defined, and there is none of the baroque hide-and-seek which we observed in the Ludovisi sarcophagus and which reappears in the equestrian figure of the emperor Anastasius (491–518

[1] The same distinction of poise is made as early as the fourth century B.C. between the standing Hermes and the tiptoe Thanatos on the drum from the Artemision at Ephesus.

[2] Delbrueck, *Consular-Diptychen*, nos. 51-2.

a.

b.

V. IVORY PANELS: THE ARCHANGEL MICHAEL

a. London, British Museum.

b. Leipzig, Stadtbibliothek.

A.D.) on the Barberini ivory in the Louvre.[1] Here the emperor's horse, seen in three-quarter view, seems ready to prance out of the frame; and the relief is so high that a barbarian is almost hidden behind the emperor's lance, his head being visible only when viewed obliquely, from the right. This baroque composition is quite exceptional in late-antique relief. As a rule, the figure is either outlined in the classical manner against a neutral ground, or isolated as a clearly distinguishable unit against a dark cave of shadow like the figures on Asiatic sarcophagi.

Nearly all the late-antique methods of composition can be studied on a single monument, the ivory throne associated with the name of archbishop Maximian and now in Ravenna.[2] This famous and much-discussed work is generally ascribed to the middle of the sixth century and is supposed to have been made either in Syria, on account of its vine decoration, or in Alexandria, by reason of certain iconographical details.[3] But as the style is so exceedingly mixed, and as in some respects it closely resembles the Barberini ivory, the throne may well have been produced at Constantinople in an atelier which contained workmen with different traditions from various parts of the eastern empire. At least four different artists seem to have worked on the

[1] Delbrueck, *Consular-Diptychen*, no. 48.

[2] Cf. Focillon, *Art des sculpteurs romans*, p. 65 f.

[3] In favour of Syria: Wulff. In favour of Alexandria: Ainalov, Diehl, Leclercq, Graeven, Dütschke. Summary of arguments on both sides by Baldwin Smith in *AJA*. xxi. (1917), pp. 22 ff. He decides in favour of Alexandria.

Plate VI opp. p. 48

throne: (*a*) the carver of the front panels, which contain the Evangelists and St. John the Baptist; (*b*) the carver of the Joseph scenes; (*c*) the carver of the New Testament scenes on the back of the throne; and (*d*) the carver of the ornamental bands. As each of these artists has a very pronounced style, and as together they cover most of the prevailing manners of the period, an attempt to analyse them briefly may help us to realise the contrasting aims of late-antique art. (*a*) is an artist with Asiatic and Syrian sympathies. The *homme-arcade* scheme takes us back at once to the tradition of the Lycian sarcophagi. The alternation of wide and narrow, taller and shorter panels is a reminiscence of the baroque architecture of the second century, which, as we saw, may be derived from the scenic conventions of the Antiochene theatre.[1] The figure of St. John is of the ascetic Syrian type; while the connexion of the Evangelists with ancient poets and philosophers, the bearded pedants of Antioch who excited the animosity of the emperor Julian,[2] is at all events conceivable. The architectural settings as well as the physical types are akin to those of a diptych with figures of Christ and the Virgin and Child, now in Berlin,[3] though the carver of the throne is the more vigorous artist of the two. Coarser provincial specimens of the same tradition are the bookcovers in Paris[4] and at Etchmiadzin[5] in Armenia, a number of cylindrical boxes

[1] Cf. Strzygowski in *JHS*. xxvii. (1907), pp. 115 ff.
[2] See his satire *Misopogon* (or *Anti-Beaver*): ed. Teubner, pp. 433 ff.
[3] Vöge, *Elfenbeinbildwerke*, no. 2.
[4] Peirce and Tyler, *L'art byzantin*, ii. pl. 169.
[5] Strzygowski in *Byz. Denkm*, i. (1891), pl. i.

(*pyxides*), one of which is in the British Museum,[1] and panels in the Musée de Cluny,[2] the Fitzwilliam Museum at Cambridge,[3] and elsewhere. At certain points artist (*a*) approaches artist (*b*), the carver of the Joseph scenes; but these resemblances are probably due to contact in the same workshop, for fundamentally their attitude to form is quite different. (*b*) is perhaps an Egyptian; his interest in the story of Joseph rather suggests it. On the other hand, he has a marked liking for Persian dress, a trait which he shares with the authors of the Barberini ivory[4] and the British Museum box with the martyrdom of St. Menas; and his rather violently dramatic style is not Alexandrian. The arrangement of his figures in deep box-like niches is curiously reminiscent of Graeco-Buddhist art of N.W. India,[5] as are also the swept-back hair and heavy eyelids; and as ivory, the substance of his art, was derived from India, it is possible that this artist may have seen some oriental carvings of the Gandhara type. By comparison (*c*), the author of the New Testament scenes, is a much tamer artist; his treatment is coarser, more pictorial, and in detail more Hellenistic, though he habitually uses the oriental bird's eye perspective which (*b*) had avoided. The fourth hand (*d*) is responsible for the decorative bands. The craftsmanship of these is, on the whole,

[1] Dalton, *Cat.*, no. 12, p. 11, pl. 7.
[2] Peirce and Tyler, *op. cit.*, pl. 167.
[3] Dalton, *Cat. of the McClean Bequest*, no. 31.
[4] The appearance of orientals on the Barberini panel is explained by the fact that Anastasius received embassies from India in 496 and 498: Delbrueck, *op. cit.*, p. 195.
[5] Foucher, *Art gréco-bouddhique du Gandhâra*, i. figs. 181, 200, 208, etc.

higher than that of the figure-subjects. It consists of elaborate vine-scrolls with animals of various kinds in their convolutions. This type of ornament makes its appearance in the first century of the empire[1] and becomes increasingly elaborate in the Antonine period and later.[2] Here, at the beginning of the sixth century, it has become a filigree network in which the organic design is less important than the lace-like effect of light threads silhouetted against deep shadow. This pierced technique is related to the openwork art of Scythia and the north of Europe; and, as we shall see, the two strands of this tradition are reunited in the Carolingian period. In actual form the vine and animal ornament of the Maximian Throne closely resembles that of the early Islamic palace-façade from Mshatta[3] in the Syrian desert, now reconstructed in Berlin, a building probably of the early eighth century; and this corroborates the other evidence for a Syrian origin of at least parts of the throne's decoration. It must be repeated, however, that the total effect is extremely hybrid: the architectural scheme of the front is Anatolian and the vine-ornament is Iranian in origin, while there are suggestions from India and Persia in the Joseph scenes, and from Egypt in the choice of subject and in some of the iconographical details. So eclectic a work, therefore, is more likely to have been made in

[1] Flavian slab from the Roman Forum: Strong, *Scultura romana*, i. p. 122, fig. 77. Relief from the Monument of the Haterii: *ibid.*, p. 130, fig. 83.

[2] A vine, with cupids vintaging, is found as filling-pattern on the Attic sarcophagus in the atrium of S. Lorenzo fuori le Mura in Rome: Rodenwaldt in *JdI.* xlv. (1930), pp. 116 ff., pls. 516.

[3] Creswell, *Early Muslim Architecture*, pp. 365 ff. and pls. 63-78.

Byzantium than anywhere else in the eastern Mediterranean.

With all their differences the figure-compositions on the throne of Maximian continue in essentials the antique tradition, both in their detail and in their general attitude to spatial relations. At the same period, however, we observe the triumph of quite another tradition, the hieratic; the effect of this, already studied in mosaic, can also be observed in ivory-carving from about the middle of the fifth century. We have seen a hint of its influence in the hovering pose of the British Museum Archangel. At the beginning of the sixth century it invades even the secular portraiture of the consuls on the diptychs[1] which they distributed on assuming office. There is a general resemblance between all these official effigies. The dignitary is seated on a chair of state, with a napkin in his hand, as though about to signal for the games to begin. Behind him, on either side, are often allegorical figures of Rome and Constantinople. All are rigidly frontal, and stare straight ahead with a fixed hypnotic gaze; immovably they occupy an abstract space without atmosphere and unaffected by the laws of the physical world. At their feet, but in a separate microcosm, is the hippodrome where wild beasts fight or chariots race. The contrast between the large figures at the top and the toy-like figures at the bottom is a symptom of the change from the perceptual, naturalistic art of the Graeco-Roman world to the conceptual, transcendental art of the Orient and medieval Europe. The convention by

Plate VII opp. p. 62

[1] Delbrueck, *Consular-Diptychen*, nos. 9 ff.

which figures nearer to the spectator than those in the middle distance are shown on a smaller, instead of a larger scale, has been called "inverted perspective";[1] it is seen on the Sasanian rock-carvings at Taq-i-Bostan (*c.* 620 A.D.),[2] and is the regular procedure in Mesopotamian art. In earlier Roman imperial art secondary subjects are often shown on a smaller scale in a sort of *predella* at the bottom of the composition: for example, the barbarian prisoners on the *gemma augustea* in Vienna.[3] This persists in late-antique art, and so into the Middle Ages. But in the diptychs, as earlier on the reliefs of the obelisk-base in the Hippodrome at Constantinople,[4] the discrepancy of scale occurs within the same tract of space; it is not conditioned by any aesthetic requirement and expresses rather an ethical, or even simply a social, standard of values. This tendency to make the ruler larger than his subjects, divine beings larger than human beings, is naturally one which appealed to the hierarchical imagination of the Middle Ages.

The development of the hieratic style, which we have studied in mosaics at Salonica and Ravenna and in ivory-carvings from various parts of the eastern Mediterranean world, was interrupted at Byzantium by the iconoclastic disturbances of the eighth and

[1] Wulff in *Kunstwissenschaftliche Beiträge A. von Schmarsow gewidmet*, pp. 1 ff.; Dalton, *East Christian Art*, pp. 162, 188, 229, 269. Wulff's conclusions are disputed by Doehlemann in *Rep. f. Kunstwissenschaft*, xxxiii. (1910), pp. 85 ff. See below, pp. 187 ff.

[2] Sarre, *Kunst des alten Persiens*, pls. 86-8.

[3] Eichler and Kris, *Kameen*, no. 7, pl. 4. Strong, *Scultura romana*, i. p. 85, fig. 57.

[4] Delbrueck, *Spätantike Kaiserporträts*, pp. 185 ff., pls. 85-8, figs. 64-6.

VI. FRONT OF THE IVORY THRONE OF MAXIMIAN
Ravenna, Palazzo Arcivescovile.

ninth centuries;[1] and its revival and triumph in the Macedonian period falls outside the scope of this book.[2] But while it was overshadowed in the east, it flourished in Rome, where the apse-mosaics of a number of churches still show the evolution of this oriental style and help us to reconstruct the sixth- and seventh-century compositions in Constantinople which were destroyed by the iconoclast zealots of the Isaurian period.

One of the few mosaics which survived the burning of S. Demetrius at Salonica in 1917 is the composition of the patron between the two donors of his church.[3] This important document dates from the first half of the seventh century (after 617), and is thus about two generations later than the processional mosaics of S. Apollinare Nuovo at Ravenna. The tone has greatly changed in this comparatively short time. The atmosphere is extremely ascetic and other-worldly: the faces of all three figures are swarthy, emaciated, and intense; and their bodies have lost all density under the flat geometric folds of their garments. By comparison the Ravenna mosaics appear quite frivolous and mundane. The same exalted spirit pervades the rows of eight saints in the Oratory of St. Venantius in the Lateran Baptistery (A.D. 642–9),[4] though the method of representation is slightly less abstract; and similar arrangements occur in other Roman churches of the seventh, eighth, and

[1] Cf. Ostrogorsky, *Studien zur Geschichte des byzantinischen Bilderstreites*.
[2] Cf. Byron and Talbot-Rice, *Birth of Western Painting*, pp. 77 ff.
[3] Kömstedt, *Vormittelalterliche Malerei*, fig. 119.
[4] *Ibid.*, figs. 120–22.

ninth centuries.[1] The presence of this exotic style in Rome is due to various contingencies, such as the Syrian nationality of several of the popes of this period, the influx of refugees from Byzantium owing to the iconoclast disturbances, and possibly also from Egypt and North Africa as a result of the Moslem conquests.[2] It should be realised that the influence of this hieratic style was limited in the west to Italy; and that Italy was not one of the chief formative centres in the period which especially concerns us. In so far as we are now able to judge, the influence of the monumental art of the Roman churches on the development of Carolingian painting was very slight. Their effect was not easily transplantable; their style was too abstract and presupposed too high a degree of aesthetic culture, too great a familiarity with figure-representations to be very serviceable to a people who needed primarily a simple didactic narrative art. Thus although the hieratic style was the vehicle for some of the most sublime inventions of medieval painting, and although in its minor manifestations—especially in portraiture—it exercised a powerful and direct influence on Carolingian art, yet on the whole it was less immediately useful in the formation of the western tradition than the more prosaic and commonplace illustrative style which early Christian artists had taken over from the popular descriptive art of the Roman Empire.

For the last fifty years discussion has raged round

[1] See Wilpert, *Römische Mosaiken und Malereien der kirchlichen Bauten vom iv-xiii Jahrhundert*; van Marle, *La peinture romaine au moyen-âge*, pp. 52 ff.
[2] Avery in *Art Bulletin*, vii. (1924-5), pp. 131 ff.

the origins of Christian art.[1] These have been sought in the Roman catacombs, among the Jewish communities of Alexandria and Antioch, in the pilgrim-centres of the Holy Land, and as far afield as Mesopotamia and Armenia. This conflict of opinion has grown all the more intense with the increasing desire to find a single source for the Christian iconographic tradition. Only now is it beginning to be recognised that, after all, there was no single source: that Christianity started among a people who had no figure-art, and that as it spread among peoples who were accustomed to visualise their sacred mythology in concrete shapes, it adopted and transformed the pictorial traditions of each region it conquered. There never was a uniform Christian style at any period; from the moment that Christianity ceased to be a Palestinian sect, it learned to speak the language of its converts. The meaning of Pentecost seems to have escaped the majority of Christian archaeologists.

In Rome itself, when the Christians emerged in triumph from the shadow of the Diocletianic persecutions, their art was not essentially different from that of the pagans whom they superseded in the highest places of the state. Indeed, it had been a matter of policy to hide their sacred symbols behind the innocuous commonplaces of Roman decorative art. The rebus of the fish, the letters of whose Greek name spelled the initials of Jesus Christ; the peacock,

[1] For a useful summary of the results of Christian archaeology in this period, see von Schlosser, *Ueber einige geschichtliche Voraussetzungen der mittelalterlichen Kunstsprache*, in *Festschrift für Hermann Egger*, pp. 13 ff. It pointedly ignores, however, the work of Strzygowski, for which see the polemical discussions and the bibliographies in his own books.

whose flesh was believed never to decay, and which therefore signified incorruption; cupids gathering the vintage of the Lord; the Apostles as philosophers; Christ as Apollo or Orpheus or the Good Shepherd: all these figures of catacomb-art were intentionally ambiguous.[1] Their sacred meaning was known only to the initiated; the profane eye saw only the stock motifs of Hellenistic decoration.

It is not surprising, therefore, that the official recognition of the Church by the Roman state did not necessarily imply an abrupt change in either the form or even the content of the art which celebrated it. The new iconography was not elaborated in a day; and in Rome and the west a long period of experiment and inconsistency was needed before the canonical forms could be fixed by authority. It is probable that in Palestine, and also in Mesopotamia, where Christianity had been tolerated by the Sasanian government some while before it was accepted in the Roman Empire, some sort of Christian pictorial tradition had already come into existence; but our information about it is extremely scanty. There are traces of it in artistically insignificant objects, like pilgrim-flasks; but no specimens of monumental art of this primitive period have survived.

One of the earliest existing schemes of monumental art in Christian Rome is the mosaic-decoration of the Mausoleum of Santa Costanza[2] on the Via Nomentana. In the apse is Christ between SS. Peter

[1] Wilpert, *Malereien der Katakomben Roms*; cf. Dvořák, *Kunstgeschichte als Geistesgeschichte*, pp. 3 ff.

[2] I.e. Constantia, eldest daughter of Constantine the Great, died in 354.

and Paul,[1] in a landscape with palm-trees on either side, the water of life gushing out in the middle, and sheep in the foreground. Whatever the origin of these motifs may be, the forms in which they are clothed are those of the popular art of the Roman world; the figures are stunted, ugly, and undistinguished. A rather more elegant style is visible in the vault-mosaics of the ambulatory.[2] Some of these are simple geometric compositions; another consists of a strange medley of birds, branches, and utensils flung at random on to a white ground;[3] and a third is covered with a large vine, with cupids vintaging, carting the grapes, and treading them in a press.[4] These scenes, secular in manner if symbolic in intention, are of interest for the light they throw on the famous correspondence between St. Nilus of Sinai and the eparch Olympiodorus touching the decoration of a church to be built by the latter.[5] Olympiodorus had contemplated a series of profane landscapes with men hunting and fishing, but the hermit recommended a sequence of scenes from the Old and the New Testaments antithetically placed in chronological order down opposite sides of the nave.[6]

[1] Kömstedt, *Vormittelalterliche Malerei*, fig. 23.

[2] *Ibid.*, figs. 22, 24–5.

[3] This so-called *asaroton* (i.e. unswept) style was invented by Sosos of Pergamon about 150 B.C.: see Pfuhl, *Malerei und Zeichnung der Griechen*, ii. p. 864 f.

[4] Cf. the porphyry sarcophagus of Constantia, formerly in this mausoleum, now in the Vatican: Delbrueck, *Antike Porphyrwerke*, p. 219, pl. 104.

[5] Migne lxxix. col. 577 f.

[6] Strzygowski, *Origin of Christian Church Art*, p. 163 f., interprets this difference of opinion as the conflict between Mazdaean and Aramaean systems of religious art.

Within the next generation we note the appearance of a more explicitly Christian style. In the apse of the Roman basilica of S. Pudenziana[1] (*c.* 400) is a mosaic of Christ surrounded by the Apostles. In the background is a city—probably the heavenly Jerusalem—and in the sky are a vast jewelled cross and the symbols of the Evangelists. Though much restored, this grand composition still remains an impressive monument of art. Yet even here the majesty is Roman, and not oriental. It is in the direct line of the great Roman triumphal scenes of an earlier day; Christ on his throne is the Emperor, and the Apostles are his courtiers.[2] The atmosphere is impressive, but entirely of this world. The hovering cross and the fantastic beasts in the sky strike a false note, like the cupids on clouds in a naturalistically conceived Renascence picture; they are intrusions from an alien world of the imagination upon this strictly secular gathering.

The same human emphasis on the interpretation of biblical stories is conspicuous in all western art at this period, whether it be the scenes from the Pentateuch on the walls of the nave of S. Maria Maggiore,[3] or on the fourth-century sarcophagi in the Lateran museum,[4] or on the ivory-carvings which were made at this date in northern Italy[5] or southern

[1] Kömstedt, *op. cit.*, figs. 26, 28.

[2] About 400 there was a notable renascence of the imperial tradition in Rome; it is sometimes called the Claudianic revival, after the poet Claudian: see Battaglia in *Bull. Com.*, lix. (1931), pp. 131 ff.

[3] Kömstedt, *op. cit.*, figs. 37-49.

[4] Marucchi, *Monumenti del Museo cristiano pio-lateranense*, pls. 6, 14-39, 42, etc.

[5] Kollwitz, *Die Lipsanothek von Brescia*, pp. 47 ff.

Gaul,[1] or in manuscript-illustrations like the Quedlinburg Itala fragments now in Berlin.[2] The personages represented belong to the world of our experience. In form they may be the manikins of popular art, with their little bodies and their large heads; but they are the likenesses of men and women of flesh and blood, and the light that falls upon them strikes a solid frame and casts a shadow. They stand firmly upon their feet in the midst of an actual landscape; it may be childishly represented, with buildings like dolls' houses, trees no larger than bushes, and mountains that are but molehills, yet it is an abbreviated version of the world of sense, not an unearthly plane conceivable only by the imagination.

A modern writer[3] has well observed that this art is more Roman than Christian, for all its theme; and that it leads, not to the Middle Ages, but to the Renascence. In part this is true; we can feel a thread of continuity that leads from the apse-mosaic of S. Pudenziana through Giotto and Masaccio to the Raphael of the Disputà. But it is also in fact untrue, precisely because specimens of this Roman Christian art of the fourth and fifth centuries figured prominently among the models which were accessible to Carolingian copyists four hundred years later, and thus played a decisive part in creating the medieval style of western Europe.

During the first half of the fifth century the Roman

[1] Baldwin Smith, *Early Christian Iconography, and a School of Ivory-Carvers in Provence.*

[2] Degering and Boeckler, *Quedlinburger Itala-Fragmente.*

[3] Kömstedt, *Vormittelalterliche Malerei*, p. 12.

tradition in the plastic arts degenerated rapidly. As a result, no doubt, of the sack of Rome by Alaric in 410, the artists migrated to Ravenna, where Honorius had established his court some while before, to Milan, and perhaps to Lérins and other monasteries of southern Gaul. Rome itself declined in material importance; and but for the rise of the papacy in the reigns of men like Leo I and Sixtus III, would have sunk into the insignificance of a provincial town.[1] This shift in the political centre of gravity naturally involved a change in the orientation of the artistic life of the empire. As Constantinople grew in importance and Rome waned, Ravenna came to depend more and more on the eastern capital for its aesthetic ideas. We have already noticed the connexion between the mosaics of St. George at Salonica and those of the Orthodox Baptistery at Ravenna, while admitting that the plastic Roman style lasted longer in the west than in the east; the same tendency is detectable in Ravennate sarcophagi,[2] which combine the wide spacing, the formalised gesture, and the symmetrical composition of hieratic art with the solid modelling and material density of antique relief.

Even in the eastern empire, however, the hieratic style had not carried all before it; and the illusionist narrative style inherited from antiquity enjoyed there a longer, and perhaps a more dignified, life than it did in the west. Instead of evaporating in the first

[1] Cf. Gregorovius, *Geschichte der Stadt Rom im Mittelalter* (ed. 1926), i. pp. 104 ff.

[2] See Dütschke, *Ravennatische Studien*; cf. Riegl, *Spätrömische Kunstindustrie*[2], pp. 188 ff.

half of the fifth century it lasted at least until the end of the sixth century, and in the capital itself, impregnated with classical culture, it probably lasted longer. And it survived in various forms. The throne of Maximian has already given us a glimpse of the possibilities of Byzantine relief-sculpture about the year 500. A certain number of manuscripts convey some idea of the narrative painting of the same period. The medical treatise of Dioscorides exists in a magnificent copy, now in Vienna, made for Juliana Anicia, daughter of western emperor Olybrius (472), who died shortly before 527. Owing, no doubt, to the secular subject of this book, the antique manner has been recaptured with great success. The portrait of Anicia herself,[1] seated between symbolical figures of Magnanimity and Prudence, bears a family resemblance to the ceremonial effigies on the consular diptychs; but the miniatures of Dioscorides discovering the narcotic properties of mandragora by experimenting on a dog,[2] and composing his book while his artist works at the illustrations,[3] are illusionistic compositions of an accomplished kind.

An almost contemporary manuscript, also in Vienna,[4] the famous Genesis codex on purple vellum, reminds us once more how widely late-antique works of the same period can differ from each other; how much depends on the models they happen to follow; how unique each work of art becomes when an authoritative and coherent tradition has ceased to

[1] Kömstedt, *op. cit.*, fig. 76. [2] *Ibid.*, fig. 77. [3] *Ibid.*, fig. 78.
[4] Wickhoff and von Hartel, *Die Wiener Genesis.*

exist. We are aware of these inconsistencies in the art of our own day, but we are inclined to forget that they are equally characteristic of all transitional periods. The history of Carolingian art will serve to underline this fact with double emphasis, for there, as we shall see, a period of violent artistic revolution looked for guidance, not to a period of stable traditions and well-tried expedients, but to a period as unsettled and experimental as itself: the fifth and sixth centuries which we are now considering. And in the Vienna Genesis the divided sympathies of the age are clearly manifested, for it can be shown that four or five different hands have worked on the miniatures, and that each has received a different education and has distinct pictorial ambitions of his own.[1] The discrepancies of style are fundamental: the painters cannot even agree whether to surround their pictures with a rectangular frame or to let their figures stray at ease across the page, whether to paint a blue sky over their heads or isolate them in the imaginary space offered by the purple ground. These contradictory methods are employed indifferently; the one is the specific style of the illuminator, the other is a reduced version of fresco-technique. The work of the illuminators—of whom there are two: apparently master and pupil—is the more satisfactory from the aesthetic point of view, though the three illusionists offer interesting glimpses of a lost art of bold fresco-painting. Both groups of painters are naivety personified when we compare them with the

[1] Wickhoff, *op. cit.*, pp. 88 ff.; Morey in *Art. Bull.*, xi. (1929), pp. 12 ff.

artist of the Dioscorides. It is a racy, popular art, much more concerned with expressive story-telling than with abstract graces and subtleties. The manikins, whom we got to know on the western sarcophagi and ivories of the fourth century, are here too; they inhabit a vague and somewhat absurd landscape,[1] which is sometimes plausible and continuous, sometimes arbitrary and hypothetical, and always put together out of a few stage-properties of a rather primitive type—trees like large mushrooms, screens for architecture, and again the molehill mountains. This narrative style is amusing and effective enough, but it cannot be called pictorial art of a very high order.

The purple ground and the dramatic convention of figure-drawing and landscape-properties occur in two other contemporary manuscripts: the fragment of St. Matthew's Gospel from Sinope,[2] now in Paris, and the Gospels in the cathedral of Rossano[3] in Calabria. In these, as in the Vienna Genesis, we get a vivid impression that the source of the artist's imaginative rendering of these sacred scenes has been some liturgical drama;[4] this would explain the odd contrast between the spritely and natural action and grouping of the figures and the extreme convention-

[1] For a separate discussion of the landscape see Kallab in the Vienna *Jahrbuch*, xxi. (1900), pp. 2 ff.

[2] Kömstedt, *Vormittelalterliche Malerei*, figs. 80–83.

[3] *Ibid.*, figs 84–96.

[4] See Bulle, *Untersuchungen an griechischen Theatern*, pp. 306 ff., for a discussion of the influence of the stage on ancient painting; for the Byzantine period see Bréhier in *Mon. Piot*, xxiv. (1920), pp. 118 ff., and Stefanescu in *Ann. Inst. Philol. & Hist. Orient.*, i. (1932–3), pp. 21 ff. Cf. Kömstedt, *op. cit.*, p. 30.

ality of the setting. It is possible that the influence of the stage-play and the mime on ancient and medieval painting was much greater than has hitherto been suspected; our information on the subject is very scanty, but it is one which would well repay closer investigation.

In spite of their differences, these three manuscripts probably come from the same part of the world. Although the purple ground suggests that they were made for imperial use, the place of production does not seem to have been Constantinople; it is more likely that they come from south-eastern Asia Minor,[1] from some monastery in Cappadocia in touch with Syria and also with the religious centres of Armenia and northern Mesopotamia, whose influence on the formation of Christian art is still disputed, but is assumed to have been considerable.

An indication of what these regions contributed to Christian iconography may be found in the Florence MS. called the Rabula Gospels, because it was decorated by a monk of that name in the year 586 at Zagba on the Euphrates. The fact that it is dated, and signed by a Syrian monk, and produced in so easterly a place, gives the Rabula Codex an importance to which the intrinsic merit of the miniatures[2] would hardly entitle it; but as this book, or others like it, had

[1] Rossanensis and Sinopensis are ascribed to Antioch by Baumstark, *Bild und Liturgie in antiochenischem Evangelienbuchschmuck des 6. Jahrhunderts* in *Ehrengabe deutscher Wissenschaft* (1920), pp. 233 ff.; but their style hardly suggests that they were decorated in a metropolitan centre.

[2] Ébersolt, *Miniature byzantine*, p. 80, suggests that these miniatures are a later addition, of the tenth or eleventh century, but gives no reason for this, beyond the fact that they are on separate vellum sheets of a different quality from those used for the text.

a considerable influence on early medieval art in western Europe, its significance will be recognised at once. As in the manuscripts just described, the decorator of the Rabula Codex hesitates between the framed picture and the marginal vignette; to the former class belong his miniatures of the Crucifixion and the Maries at the Tomb,[1] and of the Ascension,[2] and to the latter the remaining illustrations. In style the figures are rather rough, but they are based on respectable models in the illusionistic technique, probably wall-paintings on a large scale. The proportions are normal, and the relations of figures to space are rationally contrived. In the marginal vignettes, however, a more popular tradition asserts itself.

The famous Gospels at Etchmiadzin[3] in Armenia contain decorated canon-tables and introductory miniatures which Strzygowski, who found the book, took to be earlier than the text, dated 989, and ascribed to the sixth or seventh century. Its resemblance to Carolingian gospel-books of the Ada group, to be discussed in detail below, was so striking that a manuscript of this type was taken for granted as the model for the ninth-century codices. But Weitzmann[4] has recently shown that the supposedly early miniatures of the Etchmiadzin MS. are contemporary with the text, and therefore of the late tenth century and useless as prototypes for the Carolingian miniatures, which are more than a century older. It seems clear, nevertheless, that these miniatures in the Etchmiadzin

[1] Kömstedt, *Vormittelalterliche Malerei*, fig. 111. [2] *Ibid.*, fig. 112.
[3] Macler, *L'Évangile arménien . . . de la bibliothèque d'Etchmiadzin.*
[4] *Armenische Buchmalerei*, pp. 8 ff.

Gospels, if actually painted in the tenth century, still reproduce models of the sixth or seventh century, so that in principle Strzygowski is justified and their inferential value remains considerable. Between the Rabula MS. and the Etchmiadzin MS. there are notable resemblances: in the ornamentation of the canon-tables, as well as in certain iconographical details. Moreover, the hieratic frontalised figure-compositions in the Etchmiadzin book,[1] with their round faces and staring eyes, remind us not only of sixth-century diptych-effigies, but also of contemporary ivories like the Adoration and Nativity panel in the British Museum[2] and Coptic frescoes at Bawît[3] and Saqqara;[4] it is observable, however, that in transit from the sixth to the tenth centuries the bodies have lost a good deal of plastic solidity, the drapery being reduced to a completely linear formula. In the Rabula MS. the figures in the framed miniatures are constructed, indeed, in outline, but that contour still possesses the power of suggesting modelled shapes; in the Etchmiadzin MS. they merely enclose flat spaces. The same contrast may be observed by comparing the seventh-century mosaics of the chapel of S. Venanzio in the Lateran, where the contours still retain some of their plastic efficacy, with the ninth-century mosaics in the chapel of S. Zenone in Santa Prassede,[5] where they are purely calligraphic.

[1] Kömstedt, *op. cit.*, fig. 130.
[2] Dalton, *Cat. of Ivories*, no. 14, pp. 12 ff., pl. 9. Probably Syrian, but perhaps Coptic under Syrian influence.
[3] Clédat, *Le monastère et la nécropole de Baouit*, pl. 42, etc.
[4] Quibell, *Excavatians at Saqqara*, pls. 22 ff.
[5] Wilpert, *Römische Mosaiken und Malereien*, pls. 114-5.

VII. LEAF OF AN IVORY DIPTYCH: THE CONSUL MAGNUS: A.D. 518
Milan, Castello Sforzesco.

A number of lost originals of the fifth and sixth centuries can be conjecturally reconstructed from the Byzantine copies of the tenth century made under the influence of a classicist revival inspired perhaps by Constantine VII Porphyrogennetos. Such, for example, are the Joshua Rotulus [1] in the Vatican, derived from an original of about 400; the Topography of Cosmas Indicopleustes,[2] based on a sixth-century archetype; the Paris Psalter 139 [3] and Homilies of St. Gregory of Nazianzus 510; [3] the Gospel-book 43 in the monastery of Stavronikita on Mount Athos.[4] In all these miniatures the antique conventions are observed; the figures are plastically modelled, and the landscape is coherently designed with naturalistic details and effects of light and shade. The success with which the classical style was recaptured in the tenth century is an instructive illustration of the voluntariness of early medieval art,[5] to which we shall again have occasion to refer when considering the origins of Carolingian art. Continuity of technical tradition is seen to be not so decisive as the will to create a style, provided always that the necessary materials are available.

It is probable that in Byzantium an intelligent appreciation of Hellenistic art never died out.[6] In the west, however, this tradition had a much more precarious existence. The number of accessible

[1] Lietzmann in *Festschrift für H. Degering*, pp. 181 ff.

[2] Facsimile edited by Stornajolo. [3] Omont, pls. 1 ff., 15 ff.

[4] Friend in *Art Studies*, v. (1927), pp. 143 ff., figs. 95-8.

[5] Cf. Rodenwaldt, *Problem der Renaissancen*, in *AA.*, 1931, cols. 318 ff.; Weitzmann, *ibid.*, 1933, cols. 336 ff.

[6] See Dalton, *Byzantine Art and Archaeology*, pp. 243 ff.

manuscripts and other documents was probably smaller; and these exemplars, instead of being concentrated—as at Constantinople, were scattered in remote places and were far more restricted in practical scope. None the less, a distinctly Western manner prevailed, in book-painting as in ivory-carving; and there is not much difficulty in deciding whether the prototype of any given Carolingian work was produced in Italy or in the eastern empire.

What may be called the Latin tradition of book-painting seems to have begun about the middle of the fourth century. The Calendar of Filocalus[1] for the year 354 exists only in seventeenth-century versions of a Carolingian copy; but even at two removes we can judge of the kind of decoration it contained, though naturally the finer shades of style are lost. The connexion between the portraits[2] of Constantius II and Gallus in the Calendar and the portraits of Carolingian emperors in bibles and psalters is obvious; and an equally strong resemblance may be noted between the calendar-pages with their architectural frames, and the canon-tables of gospel-books. The transition from a secular to a religious use involves only the very slightest alteration of form.

The actual style and technique of the Roman miniature of about 400 can be conveniently studied in the famous Vatican Virgil,[3] the Iliad in the Ambrosiana,[4] and the fragments of the pre-Vulgate

[1] Strzygowski, *Calenderbilder des Chronographen vom Jahre 354. Ergänzungsheft des JdI.*, i. (1888).

[2] *Op. cit.*, pls. 34–5.

[3] Nolhac *in Notices et extraits*, *xxxv*. pt. 2 (1897), pp. 683 ff.

[4] Ceriani and Ratti, *Homeri Iliadis pictae fragmenta ambrosiana.*

Latin version of the Scriptures called the Quedlinburg Itala, now in Berlin.[1] The conventions are purely pictorial. The miniatures are framed with prominent rectangular borders, which open like windows into space—the unlimited aerial landscape of Pompeian frescoes, with its high horizon and panoramic disposition. On the whole, the same conception of form obtains in the nave-mosaics of S. Maria Maggiore,[2] which seem to be earlier than those on the triumphal arch of Sixtus III (432–40).[3] The figures are larger in proportion to the space they occupy, and more crowded together; but the essential landscape features are present. In the Mausoleum of Galla Placidia at Ravenna,[4] on the other hand, the figures—except in the Good Shepherd mosaic—are isolated on a negative dark-blue ground, which, like the gold ground, is intended to suggest an abstract atmosphere.

A contrasted style, less pictorial and more narrative, may be inferred for the archetype of the Terence manuscripts which now survive only in copies of the ninth and later centuries.[5] The portrait of the poet in a medallion goes back to an early imperial type,[6] but the book-presses with masks and the scenes from

[1] Schultze, *Quedlinburger Itala-Miniaturen*; Degering and Boeckler, *Quedlinburger Itala-Fragmente*.

[2] Wilpert, *Römische Mosaiken und Malereien*, pls. 8-28, pp. 412 ff.

[3] This discrepancy of style may, however, be due to differences between the patterns which the mosaists followed.

[4] *Ibid.*, pls. 49-52.

[5] Jones and Morey, *Miniatures of the Manuscripts of Terence*; cf. Rodenwaldt in *NGG.*, 1925, pp. 33 ff.

[6] Cf. Martial, xiv. 186, on the portrait of Virgil in vellum rolls of his period.

the comedies are set in unlimited space, like the miniaturists' pictures in the Vienna Genesis and the kindred representations in the Rossano and Sinope MSS.; the explicit connexion of this unframed type of composition with the theatre in the Terence MSS. confirms the suspicion, already expressed, that the liturgical drama of Antioch may have inspired the decorators of the biblical manuscripts produced in those regions. It has also been suggested that the archetype of the Utrecht Psalter was of the same style and period;[1] and to the same general class we may ascribe the originals of the Aratus MS. at Leiden[2] and the treatise on surveying from Fulda now in the Vatican.[3] These technical works naturally contain illustrations of a more diagrammatic and less pictorial nature than books in which the figured commentary is an added enrichment, not an intrinsic and necessary part of the text; and it is obvious that the framed miniature would be a less appropriate form of decoration than the free marginal vignette.[4]

After the fifth century the illumination of manuscripts and the carving of ivories in the west become very discontinuous;[5] and the modern student is baffled both by the scantiness of the material for

[1] See below, p. 115. Bijvanck in *AA.*, 1933, col. 380, postulates an original in the style of the Joshua rotulus, which is an East Roman variant of the same unframed type of composition.

[2] Thiele, *Antike Himmelsbilder*, pp. 77 ff.; Bijvanck in *Bull. soc. franç. reprod. MSS. peint.*, xv. (1931), pp. 65 ff.

[3] Bijvanck in *Meded.* iii. (1923), pp. 123 ff.

[4] The fact that the illustrations of the Vienna Dioscorides vary from framed pictures for the allegorical portraits to vignettes for the text-figures (e.g. the coral: Kömstedt, fig. 79) shows that this distinction was well understood.

[5] See, for example, Haseloff, *Preromanesque Sculpture in Italy*.

comparison, its generally low artistic value, and the inconsequence and ambiguity of its style. Only a few objects are of outstanding importance to anyone but a specialist; and the most aesthetically interesting survivals of Ostrogothic and Lombard Italy, Merovingian Gaul, Visigothic Spain, and Saxon England are those which are due to the creative genius of the northern races. The antique tradition does, of course, persist; and we must here take some notice of its sporadic manifestations, because to some extent they helped to make the Carolingian renascence a practical proposition when the moment arrived. But it is useless to look for signs of a strong inventive spirit among the classicists of the Dark Ages; their function was to preserve, in a state of suspended animation, a manner which might be reanimated when a fresh impulse was transmitted by some exterior agent. Thus it is that many of the objects which we must now examine briefly have a rarity-value, but little intrinsic importance as authentic works of art. But being rare, and therefore curious, their relative significance must be considerable; and pieces which we should ignore in studying a period when tradition was strong and creative activity continuous now become primary documents.

Such, for example, is the Codex Amiatinus in the Laurentian Library at Florence.[1] This manuscript contains a miniature of a bearded man writing in a library, which is indicated by a press full of volumes and writing-materials in the background. There are

[1] Haseloff in *Rep. f. Kunstw.*, xlii. (1920), pp. 206 ff., considers this an English copy *c.* 700 of a late-antique original.

reasons for thinking that this may be intended for a portrait of Cassiodorus in his library at Vivarium; and the miniature thus acquires a literary association-value as the likeness of one who did more than any other single man to save classical letters from the wreck of the ancient world and transmit them to posterity. But it also has a singular importance for the art-historian, since it almost certainly acted as a model for the evangelist portraits in the Lindisfarne Gospels;[1] and we are thus enabled to control precisely the change which this picture, conceived essentially in the antique plastic style, underwent when converted into the calligraphic idiom of northern art.

The transmission of the evangelist type and its transformation from an antique to a medieval shape are further illustrated by a miniature in the gospel-book now in the library of Corpus Christi College at Cambridge.[2] This manuscript came from Canterbury, and was quite possibly brought over by St. Augustine in 597; it is therefore likely to have been one of the models accessible to the illuminators of the Canterbury school, which, as we shall see, was one of the most important in Europe immediately before the Carolingian period. The figure of St. Luke, with his symbol in the lunette over his head, is based on the pensive seated philosopher of antique art, a type which was very early turned to Christian use, as we see from the statue of St. Hippolytus in the Lateran.[3] The plastic conception has already been

Plate VIII opp. p. 70

[1] Millar, *Lindisfarne Gospels*, pls. 20, 24, 29, 33.
[2] Dalton, *op. cit.*, p. 486.
[3] Marucchi, *Monumenti del museo cristiano pio-lateranense*, pl. 40.

converted into linear form by the end of the sixth century, and into a linear form which we immediately perceive to be medieval. This quality is even more conspicuous in the small panels containing scenes from the life of Christ superposed on either side of the central figure; these are no longer paintings, but tinted drawings. The same tendency is exhibited in the treatment of the architecture and ornament; the naturalistic polychrome accessories of a manuscript like the Vienna Dioscorides are flattened and attenuated into a calligraphic pattern. It would be rash to assume that this was a Latin trait, although the book was probably decorated in Rome, for the same symptoms appear in the Rabula Gospels, where the treatment of the canon-tables is equally linear and non-plastic in style. It is possible, therefore, that the Cambridge Gospels reflect a Syrian tradition, and are not essentially a work of western art. The arrangement of small panels in tiers on either side of the main subject frequently occurs on the five-part ivory bookcovers[1] which were greatly favoured in the fifth and sixth centuries, both in the west and also in Syria and Egypt, and which were extensively copied by Carolingian carvers. The origin of this arrangement has not been clearly established. It is noteworthy, however, that it was particularly popular in India; and as it occurs on ivories which show

[1] Western examples: Bookcovers in the Cathedral-Treasury, Milan (Delbrueck in *Ant. Denkm.* iv. 1 (1927), pls. 5–6); fragments in Paris and Berlin (Volbach-Salles-Duthuit, pl. 10). Syrian examples (?): Bookcovers in Paris and Etchmiadzin (Volbach, nos. 34–5). Coptic example: Bookcover in Ravenna (Volbach, no. 37). The Barberini Anastasius panel (Delbrueck, no. 48) is similarly arranged.

other Indian characteristics,[1] and as ivory is itself an Indian material, it is conceivable that this type of composition reached the Mediterranean in such a manner.

Another important manuscript whose illustrations are exclusively linear in style is the Ashburnham Pentateuch in the Bibliothèque Nationale,[2] a work probably of the seventh century and of very doubtful origin. Northern Italy, Africa, Spain, and France have all been suggested as possible sources. The style of writing and peculiarities of spelling seem to point either to Spain[3] or to Tours.[4] The illustrations are unique in style, and are certainly dependent on some sort of oriental model. The figure-subjects are evidently derived from vignettes, probably strung out on a roll in the manner of the Joshua Rotulus; they are then fitted together into a kind of patchwork, producing an effect not unlike a modern *photomontage*. The most remarkable feature of these vignettes is the abundance and elaboration of their architectural accessories. These consist mainly of baldacchino-structures,[5] many of them with bulbous domes; but there are also long basilicas with arcades and rows of windows and tiled roofs, and in one miniature there are groups of cubical white houses set cornerwise to enhance their solidity. For parallels

[1] Cf. Berstl in *Jahrb. f. asiat. Kunst*, i. (1924), pp. 165 ff.

[2] von Gebhardt, *Miniatures of the Ashburnham Pentateuch*.

[3] Neuss, *Katalonische Bibelillustrationen*, pp. 59 ff.; Bordona, *Spanish Illumination*, i. pp. 4 ff., pls. 1–3.

[4] Rand, *Survey of the MSS. of Tours*, cat. no. 2, pp. 82 ff. (full bibliography).

[5] For the significance of this baldacchino-conception of architecture, see Sedlmayr in *Kunstwissenschaftliche Forschungen*, ii. (1933), pp. 25 ff.

VIII. ST. LUKE: MINIATURE FROM THE CANTERBURY GOSPELS
Cambridge, Corpus Christi College.

we must look to the ivory with a procession of relics at Trier,[1] to the panels thought to come from the patriarchal throne of Grado[2] and now mainly in the Castello Sforzesco in Milan, and above all to the recently discovered mosaics in the Mosque of the Ummayyads at Damascus;[3] as these monuments range in date from the late sixth to the early eighth centuries, they are contemporary with the Ashburnham Pentateuch. It seems probable, therefore, that the material from which the illuminations were composed was of Syrian origin.

These three manuscripts—the Codex Amiatinus, the Corpus Gospels, and the Ashburnham Pentateuch —were all at an early date in the possession of western monasteries: Lindisfarne, Canterbury, and Tours. They show how precarious and how artificial were the links that bound antiquity to the Middle Ages; a single manuscript or ivory bookcover bears an almost intolerable weight of responsibility. It seems as if only a chain of miracles could have preserved this tradition of a humanist representational art in a world which habitually expressed itself in a very different idiom.

[1] Strzygowski, *Orient oder Rom.*, pp. 85 ff., fig. 38.
[2] Maclagan in *Burl. Mag.*, xxxviii. (1921), pp. 178 ff.
[3] Creswell, *Early Muslim Architecture*, pp. 149 ff., pls. 36-45. The upturned pagoda-like roofs of the Ashburnham Pentateuch occur both in the Damascus mosaics and the Rabula Gospels.

III

The art of the Germanic and Celtic peoples before the advent of Christianity to the north was hardly concerned at all with the representation of human beings.[1] It admitted animal forms, and even an occasional mask, but the activities of man were excluded. Moreover, in their treatment of animals pre-Christian Nordic artists made little direct use of perceptual data. That is to say, they did not look at nature with analytical eyes and seek to imitate line for line the image that fell upon the retina. On the contrary, they copied the interior model elaborated by the imagination; and it is this highly refracting medium that converted the sensuous world into the fantastic conceptual world of early Nordic art.

This abstract conceptual style is the characteristic expression of so-called primitive peoples. But it would be a grave mistake to call the Celtic art of the La Tène period or the Germanic art of the migration-period primitive in any technical or aesthetic sense. The process of development which began in the late stone age and continued until the beginning of history is one of cumulative, if not uniform, advance towards a complete mastery of material and a perfect expression of the given idea of form. What that idea

[1] The analysis of Germanic art here attempted is based on that of Adama van Scheltema in his book, *Die altnordische Kunst*, and especially on the summary on pp. 211 ff.

was, and how it affected the subsequent evolution of Germanic art, we have now briefly to consider.

It is only in recent years that European historians of art have learnt to take seriously a style which is not primarily occupied with representation;[1] and the notion of a non-figurative art, devoid of all ambition to copy the shapes of what is conventionally called the "real" world, is not congenial to those whose education has given them a bias towards humanist values. But unless we can abandon this prejudice and accept the independent authority of non-imitative art, we shall never understand either the nature of pre-Christian northern art or its important influence on the Christian art of the Middle Ages. It seems desirable, therefore, to explain as briefly as possible, and without unnecessary detail, the fundamental principles of Nordic art and the main problems connected with its self-realisation.

The history of Nordic art is the history of a conflict between functional and decorative form. In other words, it is the story of the development of ornament from its origin as a subordinate accessory to its climax as an autonomous mode of artistic expression. This process, as already implied, was not continuous in rhythm; it consists, rather, of three successive transformation-scenes, which are laid respectively in the stone, bronze, and iron ages. In each of these scenes we note a tension between two opposed conceptions of form, of which the first may be called tectonic and the second organic. In the first the tendency is to stick simple elements together until they form a complex unit; and in the second the

[1] See Strzygowski, *Origin of Christian Church Art*, pp. 102 ff.

tendency is for the unit to evolve like a cellular structure. In the former instance, therefore, the movement is from the border inwards towards the centre; and in the latter it is from the nucleus outwards towards the limits of the area decorated. It will thus be seen that borders are composed of tectonic elements and space-filling ornament of organic elements. In each of the three stages it is always the organic principle that triumphs over the tectonic; and as the general disposition of the decorative material progresses from comparatively rudimentary groups of straight lines in the stone age to arrangements of forms about a centre in the bronze age and symmetrical arrangements in the iron age, it will be clear that in the last stage of all a very complicated type of organic design will be the result.

It is important to remember that the repertory of forms thus acquired is cumulative. Older systems are not superseded so much as transformed by their successors; and alongside the new discovery the old method survives, though in altered shape.[1] For example, in the stone age the pattern begins with groups of strokes, which yield to zigzag arrangements, though always maintaining the rectilinear quality. Curved forms arrive in the bronze age, and the rows of strokes and the zigzags become rows of circles and wave-bands; but now we have also to deal with the new principle of arrangement about a centre, with its arched border strips and its central stars or spiral whorls. In the iron age the rectilinear arrange-

[1] This process is illustrated by Adama van Scheltema in a convenient diagram on p. 222.

ment appears in the form of rows of animal heads (tectonic) or bands of interlacing animals (organic); the arrangement about a centre shows the arched border strips and spiral whorls converted into animal's head borders and animal whorls; while the especial refinement of the period consists of confronted animals (tectonic) or bilateral and reversed-symmetrical double beasts (organic). We see, therefore, that the Germanic animal-style of the iron age, so far from being primitive, is an exceedingly complex and sophisticated affair, embodying the results of at least two previous cultural strata, in each of which, as in the third and final stage, two conflicting tendencies kept up a kind of dialectical struggle. It is necessary to insist on this elaborate cumulative process, which occupied many centuries, in order finally to dispel any lingering suspicion that the pre-Christian art of northern Europe was in any way inferior in lineage or status to the Christian art which supplanted and transformed it; on the contrary, it would not be difficult to show that, as far as technical and aesthetic values were concerned, the pagan art of the north had a distinct advantage over the Christian art of the south, and that its weakness and vulnerability were those of old age, not those of infancy.

The opposition of tectonic to organic principles, analysed by Adama van Scheltema, is, as he pointed out, another form of the opposition of classical to baroque principles which we studied in the art of the Roman Empire.[1] Regarding, for the moment, the

[1] For a critique of Wölfflin's theory in this context, see *Altnordische Kunst*, pp. 230 ff.

Nordic art of the bronze and iron ages as a single aesthetic phase, we perceive the gradual substitution of baroque for classical values. The bronze age offers us, in a sense, the classical geometric art midway between the primitive art of the stone age and the baroque art of the iron age. And as the iron age, and therefore the baroque phase of Germanic art, are our immediate concern, as directly anticipating in time the earliest Christian art of northern Europe, we must consider how the baroque traits in Nordic art compare with the parallel tendencies in Mediterranean art, how the two traditions react upon each other, and why the North seems to be especially propitious to the development of baroque forms.

It has often been remarked by students of German art that certain modes of expression tend to recur throughout its history, especially at moments when its growth is relatively undisturbed by alien influences from the Mediterranean world. Between the intricacies of the Teutonic animal-style of the migration-period, the complexities of certain Carolingian and Ottonian book-paintings, and the intensity of religious sculpture in the fifteenth and again in the seventeenth centuries, it is possible to trace a community not only of sentiment, but of actual formal method. Worringer has called this Teutonic proclivity *geheime Gotik*,[1] and has tried to explain it as a racial tendency which periodically reasserts itself when the alien classical discipline from the South is temporarily relaxed. Adama van Scheltema, on the other hand, finds the racial interpretation unaccept-

[1] See *Formprobleme der Gotik* (ed. 1927), pp. 27 ff.

able, and offers an alternative explanation based upon the biological metaphor of cyclic repetition.[1] But he does not account for the fact, which he notes, that the Teutonic genius seems to operate most freely at the end of his cycles; or in other words, say why it instinctively prefers baroque modes of expression. It would appear, therefore, that both Worringer's racial theory and Adama van Scheltema's cyclic theory are based on half-truths; and that the historical fact implies the coincidence of these two tendencies. The application of the general style-cycle to the particular Teutonic case should not blind us to the fact that baroque is not peculiar to the Teutonic genius, and also to its corollary that the Teutonic genius has other constants—and especially that *Sachlichkeit* which we recognise alike in the paintings of Holbein and the architecture of Gropius.

The defect of Adama van Scheltema's interpretation of Nordic art is that it is too abstract and too schematic. The process it describes appears to be taking place in a laboratory under carefully controlled conditions, not among all the accidents and contingencies of the real world. For example, his famous tension between the tectonic and organic principles is treated as if it were a natural law inherent in the behaviour of things; he leaves this curious polarity unexplained, whereas actually it is one of the most interesting features not only of pre-Christian Nordic art, but of all Germanic art down to the present day. The characteristic conflict between *Expressionismus* and *Sachlichkeit* in twentieth-century German painting

[1] *Op. cit.*, pp. 243 ff.

is only the latest aspect of this agelong dispute;[1] and this persistence of a divided aim suggests that only a racial inconsistency can be its cause. Fortunately, such an explanation is not far to seek.

At about the same time as Greek art was taking shape in the Mediterranean area (seventh–sixth centuries B.C.), two other cultures were engaged in forming a distinctive style: the Scythian to the north-east and the Celtic to the north-west.[2] The main element in the Scythian style is the animal and in the Celtic style the geometric strip-pattern. In the next period these elements interpenetrate mutually; and animals appear in Celtic art, while Scythian art takes over strip-patterns of various kinds. This central-European art, which is generally called after the settlement of La Tène in N.W. Switzerland where so many of its products were found, corresponds in date with about the last four centuries of the pre-Christian era.[3] Its connexion with the decorative art of Greece and Etruria is obvious; lotus and palmette and other classical motifs are borrowed and celticised; and from the east come animals based on the Graeco-Persian ibexes and other beasts which form the handles of metal vases like those in the Oxus Treasure.[4] But the use to which these borrowed elements are put, not less than the voluntary restrictions in the choice

[1] Cf. Einstein, *Kunst des 20. Jahrhunderts*, p. 153. See below, p. 211 f.

[2] Cf. Brehm, *Ursprung der germanischen Tierornamentik*, in Strzygowski, *Der Norden in der bildenden Kunst Westeuropas*, pp. 92 ff. See also the more detailed treatment of Salin, *Altgermanische Tierornamentik*.

[3] See Jacobsthal in *Die Antike*, x. (1934), pp. 17 ff., for an excellent aesthetic analysis of the earlier phases of La Tène art.

[4] Dalton, *Treasure of the Oxus*², no. 116, pl. 1.

of motifs borrowed, may serve to emphasise the essential difference between the Nordic and the Mediterranean attitude to form. This is nothing less than the distinction between monumental and non-monumental art. The Greek conception of form was monumental. Marble architecture and life-size statues of human beings set the scale for every creation of Greek art; and even the smallest objects bear some reference to this chosen standard. But in Celtic art these monumental forms do not exist. There are no buildings and there are no statues to set a scale to which the so-called minor arts must conform; and in consequence the minor arts cease to be minor and become their own standard of reference. One reason for this is social. The Greeks developed an urban civilisation which encouraged monumental forms of expression; whereas the Celts retained their tribal structure and their mobility, with the result that their artistic productions had perforce to be small, portable, and so non-monumental. Even so, of course, they might have created an art which centred round the human figure, like certain African tribes, whose art is often astonishingly monumental. But they did not. Like the Scythians, their neighbours to the east, and the Germans, their successors in the middle of Europe, they shrank from committing themselves to human likenesses. This renunciation is of extreme importance, not only for its negative but also for its positive results. The negative consequence will presently concern us; but it is a historical sequel, not something intrinsically significant. The positive consequence, however, is that this avoidance of the human figure has an actual effect on the treatment of the ornamental and animal forms. The discipline of studying and reproducing the human body, with its symmetrical structure, sharply defined forms, and well co-ordinated proportions, is bound to react on the artist's method of approaching all else that his art embraces. On the other hand, an art which sets out from the observation of the rapid movement of animals and the intricacies of vegetable forms will as naturally become involved, restless, and dynamic as its humanly aimed rival is clear, calm, and static. The motives which impelled Mediterranean man to imitate human shapes and Nordic man to ponder on animal shapes are doubtless deeply buried in racial psychology, but the effect of that impulse is clear enough.

It will be observed that the aesthetic result of the Mediterranean artist's absorbing interest in the human body is the classical norm of symmetry, clarity, and harmony, whereas the aesthetic result of the Nordic artist's devotion to animal motifs and geometrical complexes is the baroque principle of asymmetry, obscurity, and discord. We are thus brought back to Worringer's position that classic and baroque are the result of racial, or at least climatic, antinomies. But as in all historical processes the interdependence of cause and effect makes it easier to note tendencies than to formulate principles, so here the most we are entitled to do is to call attention to certain persistent proclivities in Nordic art which from time to time lead to such phenomena as the Teutonic animal-style, late Gothic architecture and sculpture, certain aspects of rococo, and to analogous phases of modern decorative art. It is clear that no continuity of craft-tradition will explain these periodic reassertions; and we are forced to conclude that some regional influence, whether of landscape or climate, exercises a pressure constant in itself, though meeting with a varying degree of resistance.

In his book on Romanesque sculpture[1] M. Focillon makes a distinction between two conceptions of space as the primary condition of plastic art which has a bearing on the difference between Nordic and Mediterranean art, and which it is convenient to mention here, since it provides us with a ready test for the respective attitudes of the Germanic and the Graeco-Roman artist to the material of his art. He calls one conception of space *espace-limite* and the other *espace-milieu*. The first means the notion of space as conterminous with the physical boundaries of the object; and the second means the notion of space as the ideal frame in which the object is situated and with reference to which it is calculated. This distinction is most simply illustrated from architecture. The type of structure conceived as *espace-limite* is the Egyptian pyramid;[2] its whole meaning is derived from its mass, its objectivity, its need to be looked at from the outside. The type of structure conceived as *espace-milieu* is the Gothic cathedral; its meaning is expressed not so much by its physical members as by the intervals which those members

[1] *L'art des sculpteurs romans*, pp. 23 ff.

[2] Cf. Riegl, *Spätrömische Kunstindustrie*², pp. 36 ff.

span. The primary physical quality of *espace-limite* is opacity and the primary physical quality of *espace-milieu* is transparency. By extension this distinction can be made to apply to sculpture or any plastic object, and metaphorically also to painting.

It will at once be evident that in this new antithesis of *espace-limite* and *espace-milieu* we encounter the classic-baroque, and hence the Mediterranean-Nordic antithesis in another form. We have already noted, in describing the functions of the background in Augustan and Antonine reliefs, how the actual and tangible marble is replaced by a hypothetical and immaterial shadow. In the latter, as in all baroque designs, it is impossible to say whether the positive forms or the negative intervals are the more essential factors in the design. Both are mutually necessary; and the effect is achieved by the collaboration of the two principles of light and dark, solid and void. This ambiguity is one of the constant features of Nordic art, whether Scythian, Celtic, or Germanic; and in all three it appears in the fondness for pierced technique, the specific application of the *espace-milieu* to a non-monumental form of art. If we compare a gold plaque like the girdle-plates from the Kuban in the Hermitage[1] with the filigree casing to a wooden cup from Schwarzenbach now in Berlin,[2] and the silver sheath from the Nydam treasure, at Flensburg,[3] these objects of the fourth century B.C. and the fifth century A.D., and found in regions as

[1] Borovka, *Scythian Art*, pl. 7.

[2] Jacobsthal in *Die Antike*, x. (1934), p. 25, fig. 6.

[3] Strzygowski, *Heidnisches und christliches um das Jahr 1000*, p. 21, fig. 9; cf. fig. 10, a Siberian belt-buckle at least 1000 years earlier.

far apart as S. Russia, central Germany, and Schleswig-Holstein, have at least one feature in common: in all the effect is achieved by a skeleton-tracery silhouetted against empty space. It is as though we were invited to focus our eyes not on the physical surface of the object, but on infinity as seen through the lattice. The aesthetic result of this distant viewpoint is a disbelief in the material solidity of the object, which exists—as it were—merely to define and detach a certain portion of infinite space, and make it manageable and apprehensible.

This filigree technique, so common in Nordic art,[1] is quite exceptional in the Mediterranean area during the classical period. Apart from prehistoric pieces, whose connexion with central Europe and the Orient is probable for other reasons, hardly any of the products of Greek or even Etruscan art leave the spectator in any doubt as to whether the space they imply is *limite* or *milieu*; the former conception is expressed quite unequivocally. Only in late Roman art does this solid-void ambiguity arise; and by this time the contact with the Germanic and the Iranian conception of the *espace-milieu* is already assured.

The rediscovery of the *espace-milieu* in late-antique Mediterranean decorative art comes partly from the north via Ravenna and partly from the east via Syria. It is interesting to observe that the lace-like marble partition-slabs and openwork capitals come into vogue at Ravenna in the sixth century[2] at the

[1] See Riegl, *Spätrömische Kunstindustrie*², pp. 266 ff.

[2] Kowalczyk-Köster, *Decorative Sculpture*, pls. 136 ff.

moment when Italy became a political dependency of the Teutonic north. The actual detail of these slabs and capitals, which seems to be suggested by knotted string or plaited wicker,[1] is quite unlike anything that had existed hitherto in Italy; nor is it necessary to suppose that it was an importation from the east. An example of Syrian pierced work of the fifth century is the ivory in the British Museum of Bellerophon killing the Chimaera;[2] here we find the arrangement of figures and accessories touching at their extremities, so as to cling together in a rigid network, which has been noted as characteristic of Anatolian work.[3] The connexion between this and the openwork design of Scytho-Siberian animal-plaques, though remote, is still traceable. On the other hand, the regular geometric tracery of the Ravenna slabs has much more in common with the openwork jewellery and bronze objects made by contemporary inhabitants of central Europe.[4] It will thus be seen that the two different channels conveyed two different kinds of openwork art into the late-antique Mediterranean world. When this process was reversed by the introduction of Christian Mediterranean art into the north, this mixed tradition, itself of Nordic origin, recoiled upon the north, with curious results

[1] Baskets were exported from Britain to Rome in the first century A.D.: see Martial, xiv. 99.

[2] Dalton, *Catalogue of Ivories*, no. 6, p. 4 f., pl. 3. The mushroom-trees are akin to those in the Vienna Genesis; the miniature horseshoe arcade is an Anatolian or N. Syrian feature; and the vertically projected composition is characteristic of objects from this region.

[3] Rodenwaldt in *JdI.*, xxxvii. (1922), pp. 35 ff.; *id.* in *JHS.*, liii. (1933), p. 206 f., n. 81.

[4] Riegl, *Spätrömische Kunstindustrie*², p. 291.

for Carolingian art which we shall presently have to consider.

In the period which mainly concerns us the geometric Celtic branch of northern art is more important than the organic Teutonic. Considering that the Franks who founded the Carolingian Empire were a Teutonic people, this may seem surprising at first sight. But the explanation is simple. The Franks were Christians, unlike their eastern neighbours and enemies the Saxons; and the centre of Christian culture in the west was in Celtic Ireland, and afterwards in Northumbria. Consequently the Nordic elements in Carolingian art are Celtic rather than Teutonic: a tendency increased by the fact that Carolingian art was essentially an art of educated people, not a folk-art; and that these educated people were either Anglo-Saxons by birth, like Alcuin, or the product, like Einhard, of an Anglo-Saxon environment such as Boniface's foundation at Fulda. And Anglo-Saxon monastic art was Celtic by training.

Between the La Tène art of pre-Roman Britain and the monastic Celtic art of the Book of Durrow, the Book of Kells, and the Lindisfarne Gospels there is a gap of some six or seven centuries.[1] What was happening to the native genius of these islands during the period of the Roman occupation of Britain? Romano-British art superficially resembles northern provincial art on the continent in so far as it uses human forms and floral motifs derived from the Mediterranean repertory; but this resemblance

[1] Leeds, *Celtic Ornament*, pp. 137 ff.

lies in the iconography rather than in the actual style. In Castor-ware, for example, there is a quite appreciable Celtic flavour in the ornament and even in the bold calligraphy of the figure-subjects; this quality of handwriting is alien to the Hellenistic art of the Mediterranean with its much more positive and static modes of expression. This native propensity is still more evident in certain purely decorative objects, which, though modest in scale, exercised a considerable influence on continental art and helped materially to keep alive a native tradition amid the discouragements of a foreign occupation.

Prominent among these decorative pieces are certain small bronze objects[1] adorned with *champlevé* enamel, a technique which seems to have come into use about 100 B.C. in Britain.[2] At first only red was employed, in imitation of the coral inlay previously used in Celtic metalwork; but other colours were later introduced—blue, orange, green, yellow, and brown. This polychrome style had a noticeable influence on the decorative art of Romanised Gaul and Germany. Classical vine-patterns and other Mediterranean motifs are adapted to the new method of ornamentation;[3] but almost immediately the effect changes, and an altogether non-classical attitude to decoration makes itself felt. The altered fashion

[1] See Riegl, *Spätrömische Kunstindustrie*², pp. 346 ff.

[2] *B.M. Guide to Early Iron Age Antiquities*, p. 102.

[3] Cf. the beaker from Benevento in the British Museum (Bronze Cat. no. 2479): Darcel in *GBA.*, 1867, pp. 265 ff., fig. on p. 275. Though found so far south, this piece was probably made in Gaul; the patterns resemble those on pottery of the late first century A.D. The designs on the flask from Pinguente in Istria, now in Vienna (Riegl, *Spätrömische Kunstindustrie*², fig. 100 and pl. 6), are more geometrised.

is most evident in the respective relations of ground and pattern. In classical art the pattern and the ground are sharply differentiated, and the pattern is felt to lie on top of the ground. In Celtic ornament, on the other hand, it is impossible to say which is ground and which is pattern; the two are complementary aspects of one wider reality, like the "being" and "not-being" of the philosophers.[1] This characteristic of Nordic art is one of those baroque traits already discussed above in connexion with openwork and with plaited and knotted fillings; it reappears, moreover, in the inlaid cloisonné jewellery which was brought into western Europe and the Mediterranean area during the migration period by westward-moving tribes who had picked it up on the steppes.[2]

All these elements, different in particular but common-Nordic in essentials, are combined in the astonishing art of the Celtic revival in the seventh and eighth centuries. The centre of this revival is generally assumed to have been Ireland, which was undoubtedly the home of that extraordinary religious activity whose traces can be found all over Anglo-Saxon England, Merovingian Gaul, Frankish Germany, and Lombard Italy at this period. But the illuminated manuscripts, which are our chief documents for the study of this art in its earlier stages, con-

[1] This comparison is used by Myres, *Who were the Greeks?*, p. 498, to describe the aesthetic basis of Greek geometric vase decoration of the tenth and ninth centuries B.C. It is worth noting that this style is commonly supposed to have come south to Greece from central Europe; it is certainly not native Mediterranean in character.

[2] See Rostovtsev, *Iranians and Greeks in South Russia*, p. 236 f., for useful notes on the incidence of polychromy in the Hellenistic world and its connexion with non-Greek cultures.

tain many elements which suggest that England has at least as good claims as Ireland to have originated this style. The scroll motives of the Book of Durrow are found in England at least two hundred years before they occur in Ireland.[1] The biting animals in the same book, which are evidently akin to the zoomorphic ornament of the Teutonic north, occur in almost identical form on an enamelled escutcheon from Derbyshire. The plaitwork,[2] which is sometimes derived—for quite inadequate reasons—from Coptic Egypt, is a familiar pattern on Roman mosaics at least as early as the second century A.D.; and if not itself a northern invention, was at least current in the northern provinces of the Roman Empire. This mixture of motifs from insular and continental sources implies a centre conveniently placed to receive such influences; such a centre would be more easily found in England than in Ireland. It is, therefore, reasonable to infer that the formation of that curiously hybrid style which celebrated its greatest triumphs in the Lindisfarne Gospels and the Book of Kells took place in some part of this country where a Celtic population, retaining some memories of a Roman past, received a new incentive from the Teutonic art of the Saxon invaders. Thus we may explain the well-known differences between the styles of Lindisfarne and Durrow and Kells.[3] The connexion is undisputed; and as a rule the Lindisfarne

[1] Leeds, *Celtic Ornament*, p. 158 f.

[2] Strzygowski, *Altai-Iran und Völkerwanderung*, p. 222; Schulz, *Das Riemenornament*, in *Mitteilungen des Forschungsinstitutes für Kulturmorphologie*, iii. (1928), pp. 37 ff.

[3] See Baldwin Brown, *Arts in Early England*, v. pp. 353 ff.

book is described as a Northumbrian derivative of an Irish manner. But now that the somewhat earlier Book of Durrow is seen to have marked affinities with objects made in this country, and it is suspected that the Book of Kells is customarily dated too early and is probably of eighth-century date, it may well be that the Lindisfarne Gospels represent the Celtic-Teutonic style in its purest, as in its austerest form.[1]

According to its tenth-century colophon, the Lindisfarne Gospels were written by Eadfrith, bishop of Lindisfarne from 698 to 721. As the names of those who made and decorated the binding and wrote the vernacular gloss are also recorded, but not the name of any illuminator, it is assumed that Eadfrith was also the artist who ornamented the book. These enrichments consist of five cruciform pages of pure patternwork, six pages of decorated text, sixteen pages of canon-tables, four portraits of the Evangelists, and a number of isolated initials. The portraits of the Evangelists are derived, as already mentioned, from a manuscript of the sixth century, and very probably from the Codex Amiatinus.[2] In the original miniatures the figures were still conceived according to the conventions of ancient pictorial art; they were represented as solid bodies occupying a measurable tract of space. The colouring and shading of their garments and accessories were, indeed, less naturalistic than those in a manuscript like the Vienna Dioscorides, and a certain flattening and attenuation were already detectable; but compared with their

[1] Millar, *Lindisfarne Gospels*, pp. 3 ff. [2] Millar, *op. cit.*, p. 10 f.

Celtic descendants they belonged unmistakably to the Mediterranean tradition. In the Northumbrian versions space and solidity have vanished, and the figures are converted into linear calligrams of a symbolic, conceptual type. It is customary to abuse the figure-drawing of the Lindisfarne Gospels, and still more of the Book of Kells, as though the Celtic artist were an incompetent bungler;[1] but as technical inefficiency is about the last charge that could be brought against the executant of the geometric patterns in the rest of the book, it would be fairer—as well as more modest—to assume that here too the draughtsman was well aware of the effect he intended to produce and perfectly capable of achieving it. And as a matter of fact, the figure-drawings in the Lindisfarne and Kells manuscripts have very positive qualities which any unprejudiced student must appreciate. The contours are drawn with a characteristically Celtic assurance; the utilisation of the space is unusually adroit, considering that a Nordic artist is unaccustomed to working within rectangular boundaries and habitually thinks outward from vortices; and great resource is shown in finding new stylisations, appropriate to the Celtic linear convention, for the intricate forms of faces, hands, feet and drapery, as rendered by a Mediterranean naturalist.

The unrivalled qualities of Celtic art are found, however, in the ornamental pages. The composition illustrated here has been chosen because it combines elements from the maximum number of sources,

Plate IX

[1] Cf. Baldwin Brown, *op. cit.*, p. 354 f.

IX. ORNAMENTAL PAGE FROM THE LINDISFARNE GOSPELS
London, British Museum.

no less than for its admirable balance as a whole.[1] The central medallion contains a pattern of zig-zags evidently derived from some inlaid technique; this is sometimes described as enamel, but the shape of the component parts resembles more closely the sections of the cloisonné jewellery inlaid with garnets which the Goths and Lombards spread over Europe.[2] It is interesting to observe that the filling pattern[3] bears no relation (except axially) to the circumference; it is simply an excerpt from an endlessly repeated geometrical motif.[4] The four spandrils surrounding the central medallion contain the snake-birds which Celtic art seems to have inherited from the Teutonic north; their wings are parti-coloured, with cloisonné scales which remind us of the inlaid Graeco-Persian monster of the Oxus Treasure and its Nordic derivatives.[5] Beyond these are four square panels containing the pure Celtic spirals invented in the La Tène period and elaborated in British enamels and embossed metalwork. Between the two pairs of square panels and along the sides of the outer frame are narrow strips of diagonal fret and variations on the cloisonné medallion motif. Here we find a mixture of the Celtic fret and the Gothic cloison which bears witness to the mutual influence

[1] Fol. 94 b. Millar, *op. cit.*, p. 41, pl. 25.

[2] Kendrick in *Antiquity*, 1933, pp. 429 ff., for the Kentish variety of this polychrome inlaid work.

[3] The "refinement of design" noted by Baldwin Brown, *op. cit.*, p. 360, is actually a hasty adjustment, conceived as an afterthought, of the rectilinear network to the circular boundary and only serves to emphasise their incompatibility.

[4] Cf. Strzygowski, *Origin of Christian Church Art*, p. 244.

[5] Dalton, *Treasure of the Oxus*[2], no. 116, pl. 1.

of two branches of northern ornamental art. All the intervening spaces are filled with an intricate maze of plaitwork. At the corners and in the middle of each side are projecting tufts of animal-interlace.

The first glance at this extraordinary composition reveals nothing but a contrast of textures. No individual forms emerge: only a certain granular effect, as of naturally patterned materials. A feature very unusual hitherto in northern art is the symmetrical balance of rectilinear panels about a centre; this must have been learnt from the scheme of a mosaic pavement or some other work of Mediterranean origin. Balanced compositions within a circle and laterally about a central axis occur in La Tène metalwork[1] like the incised British mirrors and enamelled horse-trappings, but the rectangular plan is as exceptional in the north as it is regular in the south. The contrast between the close texture of the plaitwork and the wider grain of the inset panels suggests two levels;[2] and for this reason it has been inferred that the model for these rectilinear pages was a metal panel, such as the cover of the Lindau Gospels now in the Pierpont Morgan Library.[3] A similar layout, however, is found on carved stones of the same period; and no definite influence of one medium on another can be safely assumed.[4]

The pages of decorated text comprise a large and elaborately illuminated initial, ornamental capitals

[1] E.g. mirror from Birdlip at Gloucester: Leeds, *Celtic Ornament*, fig. 9; enamels from Polden Hill in the B.M.: *ibid.*, pl. 1, opp. p. 40.

[2] Zimmermann, *Vorkarolingische Miniaturen*, p. 115.

[3] Rosenberg, *Zellenschmelz*, iii. p. 70, fig. 112.

[4] Collingwood, *Northumbrian Crosses*, pp. 10 ff.

in black with some coloured filling, and broken rectangular borders. These last are a slight concession to Mediterranean symmetry; but they are neither very appropriate nor successful, and the designer of the Book of Kells was well advised to conform to the genius of Nordic art and dispense with them. For a student of Carolingian art these pages are of interest as they suggest the origin of the text-ornament in manuscripts of the Franco-Saxon school; but in themselves they are unattractive, because based on an unsuccessful compromise between the free and asymmetric schemes of Nordic composition and the rectilinear constraint of Mediterranean decoration.

The Lindisfarne Gospels are the triumph of Nordic Christian art. The exquisite sensibility of their colour, the intricacy of their patterning, their consummate use of ornament for its own sake prove the value and power of Nordic art. But its limitations as a form of Christian expression are obvious enough; and it is not surprising that this superb art, so purely aesthetic in its intentions, was an art without a future. The Carolingian renascence was not primarily concerned with aesthetic values.

PART TWO

THE SUBJECT-MATTER OF CAROLINGIAN ART

I

In the year 726 the Byzantine emperor Leo III issued a decree categorically condemning the use of religious pictures, and thus launched the Iconoclastic Controversy which agitated the whole of Europe for more than a century.[1] The source of this dispute was theological. Leo, a native of Isauria in south-eastern Asia Minor, sympathised with a puritan movement which had its origin in those regions; and it is also possible that he was influenced by the Moslem dislike of images. But though Leo and his successor Constantine V Copronymus were commonly reproached with being excessively susceptible to Arabian ideas,[2] it is clear that the iconoclasts, unlike the orthodox theologians of Islam, had no objection to the representation of human beings as such; on the contrary, secular pictures enjoyed a great vogue, and even the Patriarch's palace at Constantinople was covered with hunting-scenes and chariot-races and

[1] See Bréhier, *La querelle des images*; Ostrogorsky, *Studien zur Geschichte des byzantinischen Bilderstreites*. Cf. also Bury, *History of the Later Roman Empire from Arcadius to Irene*, ii. pp. 428 ff.; Vasiliev, *History of the Byzantine Empire*, i. pp. 307 ff.

[2] Theophanes called Leo *σαρακηνόφρων* and *ἀραβικῷ φρονήματι κρατυνόμένος*, quoted by Bury, *op. cit.*, p. 431.

similar subjects.[1] The theoretical attitude of the iconoclast emperors may be open to doubt, but the results of their policy are clear enough. Quantities of holy pictures were destroyed, and the artists who made them fled to the west, where they were received and sheltered and encouraged; for the image-breaking enthusiasm of the Isaurian emperors found little response in Rome, and Pope Gregory II blamed Leo for having diverted the people from a wholesome interest in pictures and driven them to seek consolation in "idle talk, harp-playing, cymbals, flutes, and such trivialities".[2] For the Iconoclasts, unlike the Puritans of the seventeenth century, were no kill-joys; the letters of St. John Damascene reveal the popularity of theatrical entertainments at this period.[3]

The cult of images was temporarily restored by the second oecumenical council of Nicaea in 787; and its acts were made known to the western world by a translation issued by Pope Hadrian I. But the theological subtleties and counter-subtleties of the iconoclasts and iconodules did not appeal to the objective and practical mind of Charles the Great; and his reply to the Pope is to be found in the Libri Carolini, which were published about 791.[4] The attitude of Charles and the court theologians of Aachen was half-way between that of the two contending parties in the eastern Church. They disapproved equally of those who worshipped and those

[1] Bury, *op. cit.*, p. 462. [2] *Ibid.*, p. 443. [3] *Ibid.*, p. 462.

[4] For an analysis, with extracts from the relevant texts, see Leitschuh, *Geschichte der karolingischen Malerei*, pp. 9 ff. The full text is in Migne xcviii.; Jaffé, vol. vi.; *MGH.* ed. Bastgen (1924).

who destroyed pictures. Charles condemned the adoration of images as heathen; it was nowhere sanctioned by the patriarchs, prophets, apostles, or fathers. On the other hand he blamed those who robbed the holy places of their ornaments. In this respect he took his cue from a famous letter of St. Gregory the Great to Serenus, bishop of Marseilles, praising him for having forbidden the cult of images, but upbraiding him for iconoclasm. "Painting", wrote Gregory, "is admissible in churches, in order that those who are unlettered may yet read by gazing at the walls what they cannot read in books."[1] Pictures, Charles added, are not to be compared with books as sources of edification, yet they are worth having for the sake of their commemorative and decorative value.[2]

The moderation and reasonableness of this attitude are all the more remarkable when we realise that Charles belonged to a race which had no tradition of pictorial art. Like the Isaurians and the Arabs, the Franks were unaccustomed to the elaborate paraphernalia of Mediterranean figure-art; and they might well have either discarded it as unintelligible or rejected it as diabolical. Instead, the theologians of Aachen, responsive to the classical education they had received in their Anglo-Saxon monastic schools, adopted the middle course of humanism and common sense. It must be admitted that they failed to appreciate fully the idealistic possibilities of pictorial art. They do not seem to have recognised it as God's word objectified in visible form. They ignore the

[1] Migne, lxxvii. col. 1027 f.

[2] *LL. CC.* ii. 23.

spiritual nature of the enjoyment of visual art, and the function of the artist as instrument of God's will. But it is a remarkable achievement on the part of the compilers of the Libri Carolini to have steered so successfully between the iconoclast and iconodule extremes, to have insisted so firmly on the decorative value of painting and to have done justice to its didactic utility, yet to have discouraged so emphatically any tendency to regard painting as magical. For the novelty of naturalistic representation was such as to expose the uneducated Franks to the temptation of superstitious wonder. This was the spiritual danger that caused the barbarians of Isauria and the primitive Arab founders of Islam to prohibit the use of graven images. It is a tribute to the intelligence and mental balance of Alcuin and his colleagues that they appealed to the higher rather than the lower instincts of their Frankish pupils.

It would hardly be exact to say that this confidence was altogether justified by the event. As on subsequent occasions, the Anglo-Saxons made a liberal gesture which was misinterpreted on the continent. The publication of the Libri Carolini set the theological pamphleteers in motion, as was to be expected; but few of their conclusions showed the same broad grasp of essentials as we admire in the product of the Palace School. Hadrian addressed to Charles a long *Epistola de Imaginibus*,[1] in which, among other topics, he discussed various instances of veneration shown to pictures in the early Church; and the cult of images was vigorously debated. Claudius, bishop of Turin,

[1] Mansi, xiii. pp. 759, 810.

considered thirty points arising out of the royal proclamation;[1] and his discourse elicited a reply from Dungal,[2] who cited St. Augustine to prove that there were many degrees of veneration besides the actual worship which belongs to God alone. Jonas of Orleans[3] also attacked Claudius, and underlined the didactic value of pictures to the illiterate. Agobard, bishop of Lyons,[4] sided with Claudius, but was prepared to admit the representation of historical, pastoral, and other secular subjects. Rabanus Maurus,[5] in his versified letter to Abbot Hatto of Fulda, placed painting above all the arts, but found it necessary to remind him that the painted semblance was, after all, a thing of nought, and that the spirit was the truth.

These theoretical disputes had little effect upon practice; and the publication of the Libri Carolini resulted in the formulation of a number of schemes for the adornment of churches and palaces in all parts of the Frankish realm, as well as in the collection and distribution of suitable models for book-painters and ivory-carvers.

With a few exceptions the monumental painting of the Carolingian period in the north has disappeared, or been so modified by later additions that its original condition is no longer discoverable. But a large number of literary texts indicate how elaborate and comprehensive the pictorial decoration of Carolingian buildings must once have been.[6] Einhard and

[1] Migne, civ. cols. 737 ff. [2] Leitschuh, p. 27. [3] *Ibid.*
[4] *Op. cit.*, p. 28. [5] *PLAC*, ii. p. 196.
[6] The texts are collected by Schlosser, *Schriftquellen zur Geschichte der karolingischen Kunst.*

the Monk of St. Gall[1] testify to the personal interest of Charles the Great in such schemes; and capitularies of 807, 809, and 813 give explicit directions for their execution.[2] But for detailed information as to what was actually carried out, as opposed to projects and ordinances, we have to wait till the next reign, when we are told of several cycles of wall-painting ordered by Louis the Pious for the church and palace at Ingelheim, on the Rhine near Mainz.[3] The left wall of the church, according to the panegyric of Ermoldus Nigellus, had scenes from the Old Testament: Paradise and the Fall, the Flood, Abraham, Joseph in Egypt, the Exodus, Moses on Sinai and in the wilderness, the Prophets and Kings and their exploits, and especially those of David and Solomon, the favourite heroes of the Frankish royal line. On the right wall were the corresponding scenes from the New Testament: the Annunciation, the Nativity, the Adoration of the Shepherds and the Magi, the Massacre of the Innocents, and episodes from Christ's ministry and passion.[4] A similar confrontation of the Old and New Testaments is recorded at St. Gall; the Carmina Sangallensia[5] record in much detail the treatment of type and antitype, each scene of the Old Testament being complemented by its fulfilment in the New. As we have already noted, this antithetical arrangement of subjects had already been recommended by St. Nilus of Sinai at the beginning of the fifth cen-

[1] *Vita*, i. 30. [2] Leitschuh, p. 54.

[3] For accounts of the excavations of the palace at Ingelheim, see Clemen in *Westdeutsche Zeitschr. f. Gesch. u. Kunst*, ix. (1890), pp. 98 ff.; *id.* in *Rev. de l'art chrét.*, lxi. (1911), pp. 131 ff.

[4] Schlosser, 925. [5] Schlosser, 931.

tury; though, as used in medieval iconography, the disposition of themes may probably be traced back to Prudentius, whose *Dittochaeon* consists of 49 hexameter quatrains apparently intended as *tituli* for just such a scheme of contrasted subjects from the Old and New Testaments.[1] This series at St. Gall was executed by monks from Reichenau in the time of Abbot Grimald (841–72).[2] Other artists of this period whom we know by name are Madalulf of Cambrai,[3] who decorated the refectory at Fontanelle; Rodulf,[4] who painted a reliquary described by Rabanus Maurus; and Bruun,[5] who adorned the apse of the abbey church at Fulda above the tomb of St. Boniface and signed his work with a self-depreciatory verse.

The palace at Ingelheim was also adorned with subjects from secular history.[6] On the left of the great hall were depicted the deeds of ancient kings and heroes: Ninus, Cyrus, Phalaris, Remus, Hannibal, and Alexander the Great. Opposite them came scenes from modern history: the foundation of Constantinople, the acts of Theodoric, the victories of Charles Martel over the Frisians, Pepin's conquest of Aquitaine, and finally the coronation of Charles and the subjugation of the Saxons. The influence of Orosius in this choice of subjects is unmistakable. St. Augustine had sketched out the course of history as the unfolding of a great religious drama, and his Spanish pupil had deliberately written the story of the world from

[1] Cf. Baumstark in *BZ.*, xx. (1911), pp. 179 ff. See also Isidore of Seville, *Allegoriae quaedam sacrae scripturae*, in Migne, lxxxiii. cols. 99 ff.

[2] Schlosser, 1030.

[3] Schlosser, 870.

[4] Schlosser, 942.

[5] Schlosser, 903.

[6] Schlosser, 1007.

the creation with this end in view.[1] The Middle Ages were quite content to take their history from Orosius; and the arrangement of his work provided a convenient sequence of suitable material for the painter.

Though none of these works survive, there remain in Rome and southern Italy a certain number of frescoes which deserve a brief mention, not so much because they throw any light on lost Carolingian wall-paintings, but rather because, being contemporary with the book-paintings and ivory-carvings we have to consider, they provide us with valuable negative evidence illustrating the danger of arguing from one part of Europe to another and from a known minor art to a hypothetical major art. This temptation must be resisted at all costs; and the utterly different style of the Italian frescoes from the German miniatures cannot be too strongly emphasised.

In the lower church of San Clemente in Rome[2] is a fresco of the Ascension which can be dated to the time of Pope Leo IV (847–55). The most remarkable feature is the group of Apostles at the bottom of the composition. They give vent to their astonishment in gestures of the liveliest kind; they cower and hide their faces in their hands, they wave their arms and roll their eyes with an admirable vivacity. Who was the artist of this vivid scene? Bertaux[3] pointed out the resemblance between this fresco at San Clemente and others at San Vincenzo al Volturno which are

[1] *Historiarum adversum paganos libri vii.* (ed. Zangemeister).
[2] Wilpert, *Römische Mosaiken und Malereien*, pl. 210.
[3] *L'art dans l'Italie méridionale*, pp. 106 ff.

ascribed to the period 826–43. These he attributes with much probability to the Benedictines of Monte Cassino, and assumes that this Benedictine school influenced the Carolingian painters of the north. Van Marle,[1] on the other hand, argues that it was the Carolingians who influenced the Benedictines. A comparison of ninth-century painting in Italy with that of the eighth shows, on the whole, a decline of accomplishment; the Byzantine refugees from the iconoclast persecutions had returned home, and the tradition they left behind was evanescent. Contrariwise, the ninth century in the north was immensely more expert in figure-composition than the eighth; and this outcrop of a new and vital tradition among the Benedictines, if due to foreign influence at all, is more likely to have been inspired by the great artistic activity north of the Alps than by any other movement. But in the virtual absence of Carolingian monumental art this influence must be regarded as purely hypothetical. We know, in fact, almost nothing about the style of Carolingian wall-painting.

With sculpture we are better situated, because it is practically certain that no Carolingian sculpture in the round ever existed. The only possible exception, the equestrian statuette in the Musée Carnavalet, will be discussed in the next chapter. Otherwise, the only Carolingian sculpture now existing, apart from some carved capitals of rather coarse execution found at Fulda, Lorsch, and other sites,[2] is in relief: ivory-

[1] *La peinture romaine au moyen-âge*, pp. 79 ff.

[2] See Meyer-Barkhausen in *Zeitschr. f. bild. Kunst*, lxiii. (1929), pp. 126 ff.

carvings and a certain amount of metalwork. It is possible that the row of stucco saints in Santa Maria della Valle at Cividale are of ninth-century date;[1] but they have no connexion whatever with Carolingian art, being rather provincial Lombardo-Byzantine in style. As much may be said for the figures on the canopy over the high altar of Sant' Ambrogio in Milan.[2] The golden altar under this canopy is of ninth-century date; but in spite of its considerable size, it belongs logically to the jewelled bookcovers and the ivories, and must be considered in connexion with them. Thus we are left with no major works on a monumental scale;[3] and in studying both sculpture and painting we are forced to rely entirely upon what would be called the minor arts in a period where we had access to fresco-painting and architectural sculpture. It must be observed, however, that this dependence on the minor arts for our knowledge of Carolingian style is probably less misleading than an attempt, let us say, to estimate the plastic and pictorial achievements of the Cinquecento from the work of Benvenuto Cellini and Giulio Clovio. In the early Middle Ages book-painting, ivory-carving, and goldsmith's work always had an importance, both his-

[1] Cecchelli in *Dedalo*, iii. (1923), pp. 735 ff.

[2] Haseloff, *Pre-romanesque Sculpture in Italy*, p. 71, ascribes these figures to the tenth, not the ninth century. This is confirmed by comparison with a group of ivories produced at Milan or Reichenau: Goldschmidt, *Elfenbeinskulpturen*, ii. nos. 4–16.

[3] The origins and influence of Carolingian architecture form a subject apart, and are considered here only incidentally where they impinge on painting and sculpture; for a general treatment, with bibliographical references, see Frankl, *Frühmittelalterliche und romanische Baukunst*, pp. 16 ff.

torical and aesthetic, which the circumstances of the age imposed upon them. Life was unsettled; and the barbarian habit of keeping one's wealth in portable objects gave these a prominence which they do not possess in more stable conditions of society. Thus although we must regret the loss of the frescoes at Ingelheim and Aachen and St. Gall, we need not assume that their disappearance is a fatal handicap to the just appreciation of the Carolingian artistic achievement; it seems probable that it was rather the illuminated manuscripts, with their gold or ivory covers, and other liturgical objects, that handed down the Carolingian tradition to the Romanesque and later periods, than the wall-painting in the palaces and abbeys. The same is true of Byzantine art,[1] and of all arts whose influence is propagated by commerce, not by the more casual, though often more intimate, contacts of civilised cosmopolitan life. The more movable an object, the wider is its potential influence.

The first concern of those who study Carolingian art must necessarily be its content rather than its form. Though the latter is ultimately of more importance to the modern art-historian, it was the former that most preoccupied the Carolingians themselves. The artistic renascence which was sponsored at the beginning of the ninth century by Charles the Great and his advisers was not primarily an effort of pure aestheticism. It was part of that wider programme of humanism which emanated from the court of Aachen. It was educational in aim. "Painting

[1] Cf. Ébersolt, *Les arts somptuaires de Byzance.*

is admissible in churches, in order that those who are unlettered may yet read by gazing at the walls what they cannot read in books." There was no lack of decorative skill among the Franks. What they needed was a discipline in the technique of narrative. They required models to copy. They had to learn how to visualise a scene. We have already observed that the Germanic peoples had no natural instinct for representational art. Even when samples were placed before them, their efforts at imitation were unhandy enough. Merovingian manuscripts show what the Franks would do without systematic guidance, the Carolingian renascence is above everything a triumph of organisation, and the credit for this is presumably due to Charles himself as instigator-in-chief, and to his executant-managers, of whom the most important were Alcuin and Einhard.

Alcuin[1] was the spiritual grandchild of the Venerable Bede, his master having been Aelbert of York, who shares with Egbert, the favourite pupil of the great scholar of Jarrow, the distinction of having made the school and library of York the centre of European culture throughout the middle of the eighth century. In 781, Eanbald, the successor of Aelbert in the see of York, sent Alcuin to Rome to receive his pallium. On the return journey Alcuin met Charles the Great at Parma, and was invited to take charge of the Palace School. He accepted; and from 782 to 796 his life was spent in organising that institution, to which the whole intellectual revival of the

[1] Cf. Laistner, *Thought and Letters in Western Europe*: A.D. 500–900, pp. 150 ff., for an excellent short account of Alcuin's work.

ninth century is due. In 796 Alcuin was given leave to retire, and spent the last eight years of his life as Abbot of St. Martin's at Tours. Here, too, he was active to the end; and the outstanding position of Tours in the next two generations as an intellectual and artistic centre is undoubtedly due to the inspiration of Alcuin. It was at Tours that the Caroline hand was perfected[1] and the revision of the Vulgate was carried out; the exact part played by Alcuin in these two cardinal achievements of Carolingian scholarship is difficult to determine, but it seems reasonable to detect in both the guiding spirit of his enthusiasm.

Alcuin was primarily a great teacher and a great administrator. His work as an original thinker is not remarkable; his verse, though fluent and felicitous enough, contains little of the true poetic feeling which we find in Theodulf, Walafrid Strabo, or Gottschalk; as a letter-writer he is surpassed by Lupus of Ferrières, that attractive humanist. But he was something more valuable than these; he possessed in a high degree the faculty for organisation and co-ordination, which had hitherto been so lacking in the tentative intellectual efforts of continental educators like Peter of Pisa and Paul the Deacon. He provided the framework and the apparatus by means of which the vital but somewhat indiscriminate zeal of Charles could achieve its widest and most enduring results. Alcuin is not a romantic figure; but the value of his work is incalculable.

[1] See Rand, *Survey of the Manuscripts of Tours*, pp. 38 ff., for the arguments in favour of assigning to Alcuin a personal share in the creation of the Caroline script.

The other great personality of the Carolingian Renascence is Einhard.[1] As a product of the foundation of the Englishman St. Boniface at Fulda and as a pupil of Alcuin at the Palace School of Aachen, he too is a child of the Anglo-Saxon tradition. His best-known literary work is the Life of Charles, a masterpiece of medieval biography whose accuracy in detail may be disputed but whose essential truth can hardly be questioned. It is not, however, as a writer that Einhard chiefly concerns us here. In addition to his political and intellectual position at the courts of Charles the Great and Louis the Pious, he was also first commissioner of works and director of the imperial workshops.[2] It is certain, therefore, that he must have played a very important part in the creation of the Carolingian style, for it is quite clear from the literary references to his work that he was not only minister of fine arts but himself a practising artist. Alcuin, who invented nicknames for all the members of the court-circle and had called Charles David, christened Einhard Beseleel, after the man "filled with the spirit of God, in wisdom and in understanding and in knowledge and in all manner of workmanship",[3] whom the Lord commanded Moses to employ in making the Ark of the Covenant. The choice of this name suggests that Einhard was famed not so much as an architect, but rather as a craftsman in

[1] See Halphen, *Classiques de l'histoire de France*, i. pp. 60 ff.

[2] See Buchner, *Einhard als Künstler*; *id.*, *Einhards Künstler- und Gelehrtenleben*. Halphen, *Études critiques sur l'histoire de Charlemagne*, p. 73 f., maintains that there was no significance in the nickname and denies Einhard any influence as an artist; this seems unnecessarily sceptical.

[3] *Exodus* xxxi. 2 ff.

metal and as a maker of those small portable objects in which, as we have seen, the Carolingians excelled. No certain specimens of his work survive. Buchner associates with his name the bronze doors and grilles of the Minster at Aachen[1] and the much-discussed statuette in the Musée Carnavalet;[2] and conjectures that the "Vussin" who is mentioned as a pupil in one of Einhard's letters is none other than the famous *Magister Wolvinius Phaber* who signed the golden altar of St. Ambrose in Milan.[3] But this is guesswork. What is more important is the known fact that the workshops attached to the imperial palace at Aachen were the centre in which the Carolingian tradition was created, and from which it was disseminated; and that the guiding genius of these workshops was Einhard-Beseleel.[4]

We know a certain amount about Einhard's tastes and aptitudes;[5] and these doubtless go some way towards explaining the remarkable and at first sight unaccountable features of Carolingian style, and especially of that which there is reason to connect with the imperial school of Aachen. A writer who modelled his biography of his master on Suetonius' life of Augustus might be expected to show a general interest in classical modes of expression; and that Einhard's interest in the antique was not confined to literary forms we learn from the letter to Vulfin

[1] *Einhard als Künstler*, pp. 40 ff. [2] *Ibid.*, pp. 124 ff.
[3] *Ibid.*, pp. 5 ff. *Epist.* 56 (A.D. 840).
[4] Cf. *Epitaphium Einhardi* (*PLAC.* ii. p. 237).
[5] See Buchner, *passim*; his conclusions are to be accepted with reserve, but the material he has collected is useful. There is a French translation of Einhard's works by Teulet.

aforementioned, in which he refers to the model of an ancient temple with ivory columns, constructed according to the rules of Vitruvius, which he sent therewith to his pupil as an example of good architectural design. It is reasonable to suppose that this, or another such, model is responsible for the classical form of the canon-tables and other architectural settings to the miniatures in Carolingian manuscripts. The mere study of Vitruvius, however, unless in some ancient illustrated edition which has not been preserved, would hardly account for the sudden and successful resuscitation of the antique style about the year 800 both in book-painting and ivory-carving. This can only be explained as a deliberate act of policy, probably conceived by a single mind. The mind most likely to have conceived it was Einhard's.

As an enthusiastic admirer of the antique style Einhard may have set about his creative activity in either or both of these ways: he may have collected manuscripts and carvings from different sources for the benefit of his pupils in Aachen; or he may have sent the pupils themselves to Rome or elsewhere, like the first teachers of the music school at Metz. The possibility that the artists were imported from Rome or Byzantium can be dismissed; it will be argued below that in spite of an obvious classical education, the artists of Carolingian miniatures and carvings all have a pronounced German accent. The more likely of the two alternatives is that they never left the north, but copied, under Einhard's directions, the models which had been assembled for their education.

Even before Einhard started to collect them systematically, there were plenty of antique works of art casually available in the north.[1] Traders introduced them as objects of precious merchandise; pilgrims brought them home with their relics; royal personages received them as gifts from foreign potentates. There was no lack of suitable material; it had only to be concentrated, arranged, and interpreted. As Alcuin reorganised Carolingian education in the interests of greater efficiency and the better use of existing resources, so Einhard introduced method, order, and a conscious aim into the Carolingian artist's exploitation of classical models.

This conscious aim was narrative competence. The Libri Carolini had underlined the didactic value of art; and the first duty of the Carolingian artist was to tell his story as clearly as possible. For this purpose the calligraphic symbols of the Book of Kells were quite useless; they would convey no information to the uninstructed mind. And the illustrations of eighth-century Merovingian and Anglo-Saxon manuscripts were felt to be inadequate and uninspiring; their illuminators had neither the will nor the means to evolve a satisfactory pictorial tradition out of their inner consciousness. It was necessary, therefore, to go back to the late-antique models of the fifth and sixth centuries.

This is not the place for a long account of the subject-matter of Carolingian art.[2] Iconographical

[1] Ébersolt, *Orient et occident*, i. pp. 58 ff.

[2] Iconographic themes in book-painting are collected and discussed by Leitschuh, *Geschichte der karolingischen Malerei*, pp. 95 ff.; see also Künstle, *Ikonographie der christlichen Kunst.* i., for summaries and classified bibliographies, especially pp. 55 ff for the Carolingian period.

novelty is not the strong point of ninth-century MSS. Not many new themes were actually invented at this period; and the main task of Frankish illuminators and carvers was to collect, arrange, and adapt old motifs to new circumstances. It is enough to sketch here the general lines which the Carolingians proposed for themselves, to observe the limitations they imposed upon themselves, and to note where their methods differed from those adopted in later times.

The cycle of subjects from the Old Testament chosen by the illustrators of the ninth century is extremely restricted at first. If we except the Psalter, which follows a separate tradition of its own, the whole repertory of Carolingian bible-pictures, until the last quarter of the century, is confined to certain episodes of the Creation and the Fall, and scenes from the life of Moses. The same subjects were popular in early Christian art; and it is clear that an archetype of the fifth or sixth century must have been preserved in some Frankish monastery, apparently Tours. It was there that Alcuin superintended the revision of the Vulgate; and thence come the first two important illustrated Carolingian copies of the Old and New Testaments—the bible from Moutier-Grandval in the British Museum and the Vivian Bible, or First Bible of Charles the Bald, in the Bibliothèque Nationale.

The Moutier-Grandval Bible was written and illuminated at Tours in the time of Abbot Adalhard (834–43).[1] It contains four illuminated pages: two

[1] Köhler, pp. 13 ff.

with scenes from the Old Testament and two with scenes from the New. Only the Old Testament pictures are narrative; they deal with the story of Adam and Eve and with the Exodus. The New Testament compositions are a Christ in glory surrounded by the Evangelists and their symbols, and an Apocalyptic subject. The Vivian Bible, which is somewhat later (844–51), contains the same four subjects, and four others: scenes from the lives of St. Paul and St. Jerome, a composition of David playing the harp, and a dedication-picture which shows Abbot Vivian presenting his bible to Charles the Bald. Though not identical in detail, the four subjects which occur in both books are so much alike that they must undoubtedly have been copied from the same archetype. Köhler has produced many ingenious and convincing arguments to show that this archetype must have been made in the second half of the fifth century, and have reflected the anti-Manichean propaganda of Leo the Great. Both the insistence on the importance of Old Testament themes (which the Manichees had been at pains to deny) and the stylistic arrangement of the episodes in strips make such a dating probable. What seems less certain is the assumption that the Majestas is also a creation of the fifth century. The Apocalyptic imagery may possibly belong to the Leonine cycle; but it is doubtful whether the hieratic enthroned Christ in a mandorla, with the Evangelists and their symbols grouped round in a completely non-representational manner, can be so early. This subject will be considered in the next chapter, in connexion with the whole problem of the effigy, which is quite distinct from the problem of narrative. It is questionable, therefore, whether the Moutier-Grandval Bible, as it stands, can be an integral copy of the Leonine Bible, though it may very well derive its narrative material from that source.

The Vivian Bible,[1] though also drawing upon iconographic themes of the fifth century, is even more certainly not an integral reproduction of a fifth-century book. The scenes from the life of St. Jerome may well come from an early illustrated Vulgate; and in style the Pauline episodes look like ninth-century rearrangements of a western composition of the fifth century. But the David-composition and the dedication-picture, which are variations of the effigy-type and as such will be discussed later, have nothing to do with a mid-fifth-century illustrated book.

The third important Carolingian bible, that of San Callisto now in the Convent of St. Paul without the walls in Rome,[2] is a generation later than the two Tours bibles and was written by one Ingobert after 880 for Charles the Fat. Its iconography is much richer than that of the Moutier-Grandval and Vivian books, and certain similarities to the Ashburnham Pentateuch suggest that the artist had access to a wider range of archetypes than the Tours illuminators. He was, in any case, a man of highly eclectic tastes, for in addition to the Pentateuch scenes, the

[1] Köhler, pp. 27 ff.

[2] Westwood, *The Bible of the Monastery of St. Paul near Rome described and compared with other Carlovingian MSS.*; Boinet, pls. 121–30. The connexion between its miniatures and those of the Vivian Bible is discussed by Venturi, *Storia dell' arte italiana*, ii. pp. 322 ff.

Psalter composition, the imperial dedication-scene and frontispiece, and the Majestas, he also gives us the decorated canon-tables and Evangelist-portraits that originally belonged to gospel-books and a number of complicated ornamental pages resembling those in the Codex Aureus from St. Emmeram at Regensburg now in Munich, though still more elaborate.

The illustrations of the Psalter[1] fall into two main groups: those which consist of a portrait of David, with or without attendants; and those which accompany and explain the individual psalms. The former group, as we have said, must be considered with portraits in general; the latter represents a completely separate tradition.

The two most important Carolingian psalters of the narrative class are those at Utrecht and St. Gall. The Utrecht Psalter was written at Hautvillers, near Rheims, about 832. It is illustrated throughout with line-drawings in a very distinctive and remarkable style,[2] built up with rapid, scratchy, squirling pen-strokes which give an impression of vigorous life quite unparalleled at this date. But the content of the work and the motifs out of which the scenes are constructed were not invented in the ninth century. There are many reasons for conjecturing that behind the Carolingian version lie at least one, and perhaps

Plate X opp. p. 116

[1] For early medieval psalter-illustration generally see Springer, *Die Psalter-illustrationen im frühen Mittelalter* in *Abhandl. d. kgl. sächs. Gesellsch. d. Wissensch.*, viii (1880), pp. 228 ff.

[2] Birch, *The History, Art, and Palaeography of the Manuscript styled The Utrecht Psalter*; cf. Benson and Tselos in *Art Bulletin*, xiii. (1931), pp. 13 ff.

two, earlier recensions.[1] As far as the individual details of figure-type, dress, and accessories are concerned, the original might be identified as a western book of about A.D. 400, of the same family as the Vatican Virgil, the Ambrosian Iliad, or the Quedlinburg Itala fragments. The palaeographical characteristics, moreover, suggest a Latin original; the use of rustic capitals and the arrangement of the text in three columns indicate that the original was written before the end of the seventh century. On the other hand, the actual composition of the figure-scenes is less like that of the fifth-century Latin MSS. that have come down to us than that of MSS. produced in the eastern half of the Mediterranean, such as the Joshua Rotulus and a Greek psalter, also in the Vatican (gr. 1927), which, though actually of later date, certainly derive from archetypes of the fifth or sixth century. This combination of a Hellenistic landscape-convention with western iconographical and palaeographical features would seem to show that the original which the Carolingian artist had before him was a book decorated in the west, presumably in Rome or S. Italy and conceivably by a refugee from the iconoclastic disturbances of the eighth century, who combined the undoubted western elements of the fifth-century prototype with a Byzantine scheme of sixth-century classicising inspiration.

The Golden Psalter of St. Gall[2] also has the text

[1] Benson and Tselos in *Art Bulletin*, xii. (1931), pp. 13 ff.

[2] Merton, *Die Buchmalerei von Sankt-Gallen vom ix. bis zum xi. Jahrhundert* [2], pp. 58 ff., pls. xxviii. ff.

X. PAGE FROM THE UTRECHT PSALTER
Utrecht, Universiteitsbibliotheek.

written in rustic capitals when adjacent to the narrative compositions; and these show signs of having descended from a prototype with a landscape-convention not unlike that of the Joshua Rotulus. But combined with these are illuminated initials of the regular St. Gall type, as well as a portrait-frontispiece of Samuel anointing David within an arched frame; and the whole organisation of the decorative matter, like the varieties of script in the text, shows an eclectic interest in models of very different kinds and periods.

Both the Utrecht and the St. Gall Psalters agree in displaying their figure-subjects as marginal vignettes, not as closed compositions with a frame.[1] The same feature is found in the contemporary Byzantine MS. called the Khludov Psalter,[2] now in Moscow, a book which is supposed to represent the popular monastic tradition, not the hieratic tradition of the court as exhibited in the Paris Psalter 139. It is possible, therefore, that the difference between the Utrecht and St. Gall MSS. and most other Carolingian MSS. is of the same kind; we know, at any rate, that the average Carolingian bible, gospel-book and psalter without running pictorial commentary were closely connected with the Palace School and that their style was controlled by fairly rigid conventions. The MSS. produced outside this circle are various, casual, and often rather crude; but they show a liveliness of mind and an independence of convention which

[1] There are signs that the vignettes of The Utrecht Psalter were copied from framed originals: see Benson and Tselos, *op. cit.*, p. 38.

[2] See Malicky in *II. Recueil Uspensky*, ii. pp. 235 ff.

makes them seem refreshing after long contact with the accomplished but often rather airless products of the palace-tradition. The Utrecht Psalter is the earliest in date of these free-lance performances; but it is followed closely by the Drogo Sacramentary, in some respects the most remarkable of all Carolingian illuminated MSS.; and later we encounter the illustrated Apocalypses[1] of Trier and Cambrai and Valenciennes which are not so much products of Carolingian art as belated survivors of eighth-century book-painting. Among these we may include the psalter from Corbie at Amiens[2] and perhaps also the much-discussed Stuttgart Psalter,[3] which is usually ascribed to the tenth century but which might be more probably classified among what we may call the non-Carolingian Frankish book-paintings of the ninth century.

Plate XI opp. p. 122

The Drogo Sacramentary was written for the prelate of that name who was bishop of Metz from 826 to 855, and is now in the Bibliothèque Nationale.[4] It is notable both for the iconography and the style of its illustrations. Whereas most Carolingian MSS. show an extremely restricted choice of subject-matter and great conservatism in the treatment even of these few themes, the Drogo book introduces a large

[1] Boinet, pls. 153-9. Cf. Neuss, *Die Apokalypse des hl. Johannes in der altspanischen und altchristlichen Bibelillustration*, pp. 248 ff.

[2] Boinet, pls. 148-9.

[3] De Wald, *The Stuttgart Psalter* (plates and iconographical descriptions only; no historical commentary yet published).

[4] Leroquais, *Les sacramentaires et les missels manuscrits des bibliothèques publiques de France*, i. pp. 16 ff.; Weber, *Einbanddecken, Elfenbeintafeln, Miniaturen, Schriftproben aus Metzer liturgischen Handschriften*, pls. i–xxviii; Boinet, pls. 86-90.

number of subjects new to manuscript-illustration; these are mainly devoted to scenes from the Life of Christ, but there are also hagiographical themes and motifs symbolising the sacraments. None of these are framed compositions of the classical type. They are nearly all combined with the initial-letters, which are elaborately foliated and converted into scaffolds for the support of the figure-subjects. In style these small vignettes bear some relation to the drawings of the Rheims School as seen in the Utrecht Psalter, and like them may be derived from some prototype of the fifth century which has otherwise disappeared without leaving a trace. It should also be noticed that there is a close connexion between the style of the illuminations and that of the two carved ivory covers of the MS., which are contemporary and which between them contain eighteen small compositions of gospel-episodes and liturgical scenes. Although the ivory covers of the Drogo MS. are as unusual in style among other Carolingian ivories as the miniatures are among other Carolingian miniatures, it is nevertheless true that ivory-carvings, generally speaking, show a much wider iconographical scope than book-paintings, especially as far as the New Testament is concerned.

Like the book-paintings they are based on late-antique prototypes of the fourth, or fifth, and sixth century; and this relation of original to copy is of more decisive importance for their stylistic character than the place of origin of the ninth-century object. Goldschmidt's classification of the material into his Ada, Liuthard, and Metz groups has certain practical advantages and does admittedly correspond to certain broad formal distinctions; but it also involves associating in the same group (this applies especially to the Ada division) objects of so varied a pedigree that they have nothing essential in common. Postponing, then, for the moment our consideration of the intrinsic development of Carolingian plastic style, we may note the general connexion of archetype and copy, and observe the prevalence of certain motifs at certain periods.

The ivories which Goldschmidt places in his Ada group[1] belong in date to the last decade of the eighth century and the first half of the ninth. It is very probable that, like the Ada group of MSS. with which they are associated, they were produced in the imperial ateliers at Aachen, or at least by craftsmen who had received their training there. But it is also clear that the models assembled at Aachen for the education of the artists of the Palace School differed extensively in style and date. Some Ada ivories are copied from western prototypes of about A.D. 400, and especially from members of that group which Stuhlfauth ascribed to Milan and Baldwin Smith to Provence. The subject-matter of these panels is taken almost exclusively from the Life of Christ. Others represent single figures on a large scale and appear to be copied from originals of the fifth century, such as the Poet and Muse diptych at Monza or the British Museum Archangel. In others the frontal arrangement and the architectural setting of sixth-century

[1] *Die Elfenbeinskulpturen aus der Zeit der karolingischen und sächsischen Kaiser*, pp. 6 ff.

consular diptychs is apparent. In these the narrative interest is subordinate to the effigy-idea. All the members of this group are explicitly derived from late-antique ivory prototypes. In some cases both original and copy have survived; and we can control the indebtedness of the ninth to the fifth and sixth centuries. It seldom happens that the whole composition is taken over *en bloc*; as a rule, the Carolingian artist borrows motifs and groups and isolated figures, and recomposes them to suit his own purpose according to the principles of his own day.

In the Liuthard group,[1] on the other hand, the carvers seem to have been influenced more by pictorial than by plastic models. The group derives its name from the covers of the Psalter of Charles the Bald in Munich which was executed by the scribe Liuthard, probably in the abbey of Saint-Denis; and the close relations between these ivories and the miniatures of the Saint-Denis school makes it highly probable that the same master-designs served for both media. In any case the artists of the Liuthard group are much more independent of late-antique prototypes than the Ada school. Goldschmidt's third group falls into two sections: an earlier and a later Metz school.[2] The class is localised from the Drogo Sacramentary, but it is prudent not to insist too much on the geographical distinction. In style the Metz ivories of the second period attempt to compromise between the classical and plastic Ada manner and the baroque pictorial convention of the Liuthard group. In content they are chiefly remark-

[1] Goldschmidt, pp. 23 ff. [2] *Op. cit.*, pp. 38 ff.

able for their devotion to the Crucifixion, a subject hardly ever treated in the first half of the ninth century. The popularity of this theme after 850 is probably due in some measure to the poem of Rabanus Maurus, *De laudibus sanctae Crucis*.[1]

If we take the subject-matter of Carolingian art as a whole, it seems that we should divide its evolution into two parts. In the first half of the ninth century the artists cling closely to their late-antique models. They accept what chance has set before them in a completely submissive frame of mind. Moreover, the practitioner of each craft sticks to his last, and cross-references from one art to another are surprisingly rare, especially when we remember that book-painters, ivory-carvers, and metalworkers all seem to have practised side by side in the same atelier. In the second half of the century, on the other hand, technical co-operation between the arts becomes much closer; iconographical motifs are shared about between painters and carvers; and the whole conception of narrative which had been so dimly and imperfectly understood at the beginning of the ninth century was completely assimilated before its close.

[1] See *PLAC.*, ii. p. 156

a.

b.

XI *a*. INITIAL FROM THE DROGO SACRAMENTARY
Paris, Bibliothèque Nationale.

b. THE CRYSTAL OF LOTHAIR
London, British Museum.

II

The creation of a narrative style was the greatest service that Carolingian artists rendered to the culture of northern Europe. It was of decisive importance that a people who had originally known no representational art should have learnt how to embody their strong native dramatic sense of an event in scenic form. But this was not the only achievement of the Carolingians as heirs and transmitters of the antique tradition to medieval Europe; an equally significant act was their decision to take over the single figure, the cult-image, the effigy from Mediterranean art. This artistic genre is quite distinct from the pictorial composition, both historically and aesthetically; and it would be misleading to confuse the two conceptions by treating their simultaneous apparition in Carolingian art as a single and indivisible event. The isolated figure is considered here in its widest, yet exactest, aspect as an *effigy*, since this term will include both the portrait proper, or likeness of a contemporary historical personage, and the ideal type of Psalmist or Evangelist; and from this the concept may easily be extended to include the figure of Christ himself.

The portrait proper, as we understand the word, was an invention of the Hellenistic age which found its fullest expansion under the Roman Empire. The Hellenistic portrait was the ideal reconstruction of a personality, in which the accidental facts of nature were indeed accepted and used, though only as the starting-point for an imaginative exercise in concretised psychology. The Roman portraitist, on the other hand, approached his sitter objectively, not subjectively; he looked from the outside at the features one by one and transliterated them piecemeal into the language of art. The resulting work was both a document and a commentary, but the former aspect was more clearly defined than the latter. The Roman portrait was the exact statement of a particular case; it was as far removed as possible from the generalised and the typical. In late antiquity, from about the end of the third century, this sharp distinction between the particular and the general was again softened and diffused. As the external surface of the physical world lost its attraction and the imagination of man became more habitually focussed on an inner landscape, the antithesis of portrait and type was narrowed down until the two conceptions were finally superimposed. At this point, which occurred in the fourth and fifth centuries, a remarkable thing happened. Instead of the portrait being merged in the type, as happened with the abortive Greek attempts at portraiture in the fifth century B.C., the type was now merged in the portrait. The imperial effigy, as it appears on certain coins and medallions of the fourth century, created the image of the enthroned Christ; and in this compromise between worldly and heavenly state, it was the attributes and ornaments of this world that triumphed. For this reason it is logical to start our investigation of the single figure in Carolingian art with the ruler-portrait, since the conventions of this genre are applicable in an unexpected degree to categories which at first sight have little enough to do with the representation of real persons.

Before studying the painted effigies which are the most obvious contribution of Carolingian art to medieval portraiture it will be desirable to clear out of our way the one alleged ninth-century example of sculpture in the round, the statuette in the Musée Carnavalet.[1] This bronze was formerly at Metz, and has been known since the beginning of the sixteenth century. Its history before that date is unrecorded; and although traditionally supposed to be a contemporary likeness of Charles the Great, its unique status as a work of Carolingian sculpture has naturally caused it to be regarded with a good deal of suspicion, and doubt has often been expressed as to whether such a work would have been technically possible in the ninth century. It is certain, in the first place, that the conception of an equestrian figure would have been possible to the Carolingian mind. Quite apart from the Marcus Aurelius of the Capitol, which stood outside the Lateran for all to see throughout the Middle Ages, it is well known that Charles the Great removed a mounted statue of Theodoric from Ravenna and set it up in front of his palace at Aachen.[2] Another late-antique equestrian group, called in later times the

[1] Schramm, *Die zeitgenossischen Bildnisse Karls des Grossen*, pp. 29 ff. See also Kemmerich, *Frühmittelalterliche Porträtplastik in Deutschland*, pp. 19 ff.; Buchner, *Einhard als Künstler*, pp. 124 ff.

[2] Agnellus, *Liber pontificalis ecclesiae ravennatis*, 94 (*MGH. Script. rerum langobard*, p. 338); for the verses by Walafrid Strabo on the subject, see *PLAC*. ii. pp. 370 ff.; Schlosser, 1140.

Regisole, was to be seen at Pavia.[1] In the tenth century, moreover, the will of Archbishop Bruno of Cologne (*d.* 965) mentions an *equitem argenteum* which had been given him by the Archbishop of Mainz;[2] this shows that a representation of a mounted figure in metal, and in the round, existed not long after the Carolingian period. Another possible source of inspiration may be found among those oriental presents sent by Harun al Rashid to Charles.[3] There is, for example, in the Hermitage a Sasanian bronze incense-burner, of the seventh century, in the shape of a mounted king; it is quite conceivable that some such object may have found its way to the west in the ninth century and provided some technical hints on the casting of the Carnavalet statuette, though in style this has nothing oriental about it. Moreover, if the Carnavalet figure is not of the ninth or tenth century, it is hard to say in what period it would seem more appropriate. In detail, too, it is quite satisfactory as a putative ninth-century object. The features, with shaven chin, moustache, and hair cut all round in a straight fringe, agree well enough with those of Lothair and Charles the Bald in the manuscript-portraits; and the crown is identical with that worn by Pilate in the diptych with scenes from the Passion in the Cathedral Treasury at Milan, a work of the second half of the ninth century. Without going so far as Buchner and ascribing the statuette to Einhard himself, we may still regard the ninth-century dating

[1] Maiocchi in *Bull. stor. pavese*, ii. (1894) pp. 218 ff.
[2] Schramm, *op. cit.*, p. 40.
[3] Cf. Ébersolt, *Orient et occident*, p. 97, n. 1

as probable on internal grounds, however surprising on external. It seems impossible, however, to determine whether the emperor represented is Charles the Great or one of his successors; the features of Carolingian rulers are not sufficiently distinguishable in their authenticated portraits to make iconographical speculation very profitable. We may thus provisionally accept the traditional identification as Charles the Great.

With the painted portraits we are on smoother ground. Not only are they verifiable in themselves, but we can trace without much difficulty the prototypes on which they are based. The materials for a study of late-antique and early medieval portraiture may not be as abundant as we could wish, but at least they are continuous and adequately differentiated into well-marked categories. The first to be considered is the ruler-portrait, and then the author-portrait; these are quite separate in origin, but sometimes impinge upon each other, as with royal authors like David. From these we are led away to the image of Christ enthroned, and also—in a different direction—to allegorical personages.

Unlike the sculptured portrait, in which the person represented is a self-contained unit occupying an *espace-limite*, the painted portrait almost inevitably presupposes some sort of explicit relation between the person represented and his setting, whether material or psychological. A scenic element is thus introduced into an art which was originally concerned only with isolated facts; and the portrait tends to become a group, or at least a genre-composition.

This tendency may be observed already in Roman imperial art. Wegner[1] has noted in the antithetical *adlocutio*-scenes on the Column of Marcus Aurelius an anticipation of the Exodus-pictures in the Moutier-Grandval and Vivian Bibles; the emperor haranguing his men and Moses addressing the Israelites are treated in just the same way, with the psychological intercourse taking place laterally on the same spiritual level. This is the humanistic, democratic, antique conception. But we may also find on the Aurelian column, and with increasing frequency in later works, a different type of *adlocutio*-scene,[2] in which the emperor and his staff are centrally placed, with the audience grouped in a ring all round; here the psychological current is radiated outwards from a centre. This is the aristocratic and medieval conception; and instead of a scene, in which all the elements are of balanced importance, we have an effigy occupying the middle of the picture and subordinate accessories, human and material, disposed as a sort of framework about the central point of focus. The distinction of importance between primary and secondary elements is generally made manifest by a difference of scale. Even on the Column of Marcus Aurelius the emperor is a size larger than his subjects; and this distinction is maintained throughout late-antique and early medieval ruler-portraiture.

The decisive stages in the development of this art-form are marked by a series of monuments which may be briefly enumerated, as showing the steps by which the frankly human event is converted into the

[1] *JdI.* xlvi. (1931), p. 114. [2] *Op. cit.*, p. 109.

hieratic ceremonial fact. In early Roman imperial art the treatment is either historical and rational or allegorical and imaginative, according to circumstances. In the first case the emperor moves among his subjects as a man among men, addressing them or listening to their requests; in the second he is associated with Mars or Venus or the goddess Roma,[1] but only posthumously and after his own deification has qualified him to consort with immortals on equal terms. This convention is respected, on the whole, in the second century as well, though differences of scale between the emperor and the rest begin to creep in. The really significant changes take place in the third century. The elaboration of imperial etiquette dates from the time of Gallienus, who was the first emperor to wear a purple cloak and tunic and gold and jewelled brooches in Rome itself, where emperors had hitherto always worn the toga.[2] This tendency was checked under Aurelian, but when Diocletian remodelled the Roman court on Persian lines the use of purple and silk became canonical.[3] The first reflection of this changed perspective in art is the Liberalitas Augusti on the Arch of Constantine, a rigidly centralised composition with the emperor frontally enthroned in the centre and the people disposed in ranks to right and left receiving his bounty.[4] The influence of such an arrangement on the medieval

[1] E.g. on the Gemma Augustea in Vienna: Eichler-Kris, *Die Kameen*, no. 7, pl. 4, pp. 52 ff.

[2] *Scriptt. Hist. Aug.*, *Vita Gallieni*, xxiii. 16. 4; cf. *op. cit.*, *Vita Aureliani*, xxvi. 45. 4. See Alföldi in *RM.*, xlix. (1934), pp. 3 ff.

[3] Cf. *Edict.*, xix. 10-14; xxii. 8-15 (ed. Mommsen-Blümner, pp. 150, 160 f).

[4] Strong, *Scultura romana*, ii. p. 337, fig. 208.

Last Judgement, alluded to by Wegner, is highly probable.[1]

The all-important distinction of scale is conspicuous on the Arch of Constantine, where the seated emperor easily overtops his standing subjects, but the ceremonial dress is not yet in evidence. This appears on medallions of about 337–40[2] and in the portraits of Constantius II and Gallus in the Calendar of 354.[3] On the silver disk of Theodosius in Madrid,[4] which commemorates the celebration of his *Decennalia* in 388, scheme and sentiment alike are medieval rather than antique. Under an arcade sit the emperor Theodosius and his two sons Valentinian II and Arcadius; he hands a patent-diptych to a court-official who comes forward to receive it. But this action is purely conventional; it plays no intrinsic psychological rôle in the composition, which is therefore not a narrative scene but a complex of effigies. Between Theodosius and his sons and the official and the bodyguard there is no spiritual communion at all. The figures gaze straight in front of them out of the picture. The conception of space is equally arbitrary; the architectural setting has only one function—to divide the picture-surface up into compartments of a manageable shape and size. The perspective of the footstools and the levitating poise of the figures in front of the column-bases betray a non-antique formal sense; and these characteristics, together with the rigid frontality of

[1] *Op. cit.*, pp. 107 ff.

[2] Gnecchi, *Medaglioni romani*, i. pls. ix. 11; xxx. 2.

[3] Strzygowski, *Calenderbilder des Chronographen vom Jahre 354*, pls. xxxiv.-xxxv.

[4] Delbrueck, *Die Consulardiptychen*, no. 62.

the chief personages, make it likely that the artist of this disk belonged to a school in touch with Persian ideas—and so probably to Antioch[1]—although the actual work may have been done at Thessalonica, where the Decennalia of Theodosius were celebrated.[2]

An approximately contemporary western work, the diptych of Probianus in Berlin,[3] shows the same frontal pose and the same contrast of scale between the principal and subordinate figures, but the action takes place within a logically contrived space under the influence of antique formal conceptions. This applies generally to the western diptychs of the fifth century; but the sixth-century diptychs made at Constantinople, on the other hand, show a completely orientalised style of composition, in which the continuity of space is no longer respected and differences of scale become entirely arbitrary.[4] These formal questions will be discussed at greater length in the third part of this book; they are mentioned here because the system of space-treatment and the subject-matter of the picture are closely connected. For example, the oriental system, as found on the Madrid disk and the sixth-century diptychs, is the one usually chosen for imperial effigies; while the antique system, used on fifth-century diptychs, is adopted for author-portraits like the figures of the Evangelists in MSS. of the Ada school.

Schramm[5] distinguishes three main types of

[1] Bréhier in *Gaz. d. Beaux Arts*, 1920, p. 191 f.
[2] Seeck, *Regesten*, pp. 273 ff.
[3] Delbrueck, *op. cit.*, no. 65.
[4] *Ibid.*, nos. 9 ff.
[5] *Vorträge der Bibliothek Warburg*, 1922–3, pp. 145 ff., and especially pp. 167 ff.

medieval ruler-portrait: the investiture group, the devotional group, and the satellite group. An example of the first type may be found in the Metz Sacramentary in the Bibliothèque Nationale (MS. lat. 1141, fol. 2vo),[1] in which an emperor, standing between two ecclesiastics, receives the crown from the hand of God, which appears out of a cloud above his head. The second type occurs in the Psalter of Louis the Pious in Berlin (Cod. theol. lat. 58, fol. 120)[2] and in the Prayer-book of Charles the Bald from the Munich Schatzkammer (fol. 38).[3] Both of these types seem to be inventions of the Carolingian age, or at least not derived from late-antique patterns; the conceptions which they embody are essentially medieval, not antique. It is possible, however, that they are derived from contemporary Byzantine models. The third type, however, in which the emperor appears in his primary capacity as ruler, surrounded by his court, is based on late-antique prototypes, which in some cases can be certainly identified.

The ruler-portraits in Carolingian MSS. are of varying degrees of complexity, from the single figure to the ceremonial group. In the Lothair Psalter in the British Museum (Add. MS. 37768, fol. 4)[4] the emperor sits on a faldstool with griffin's heads and claws, wearing a chlamys and tunic covered all over with immense jewel-like spots, a crown and a fibula with jewelled knobs, breeches, puttees, and boots; he holds a long sceptre in his right hand and a jewelled

[1] Leroquais, *Sacramentaires et missels manuscrits*, i. no. 13, p. 35 f.; Boinet, pl. 131a.

[2] Leitschuh, pp. 90, 171. [3] *Ibid.*, p. 170. [4] Boinet, pl. 79a.

XII. THE EMPEROR LOTHAIR: MINIATURE FROM HIS GOSPEL-BOOK
Paris, Bibliothèque Nationale.

sword in the left. There are no attendants, and the background is a plain, dark surface without modelling or any other incident. Though the pose is traditional, there are no signs that the artist has followed any specific late antique model; indeed, the mixture of grandeur and gaucherie in this rather engaging portrait suggests that it is a Carolingian invention.

A more sophisticated likeness of the same monarch appears in his Gospel-book, a Tours MS. in the Bibliothèque Nationale (MS. lat. 266, fol. 1vo).[1] Lothair sits in the usual medieval posture with his knees wide apart and his feet close together, on a throne with a high, semicircular back draped inside. Behind him to left and right stand two helmeted attendants, whose position and equipment indicate that they are derived from the Rome and Constantinople of sixth-century diptychs.[2] The influence of the school of Rheims appears in the slightly strained facial expression, the linear handling of the drapery, and the curious little scalloped ground-lines to right and left of the throne, which imply that the scene is set in the open air. This relates it to the ruler-groups in the Utrecht Psalter and other portraits in Rheims MSS., where this *al fresco* setting for what are really indoor occupations is singularly popular.

Plate XII opp. p. 132

Plate VII opp. p. 62

An architectural setting for the ruler-portrait is seen in the Psalter of Charles the Bald in the Bibliothèque Nationale (MS. lat. 1152, 3vo).[3] The hand

[1] Boinet, pl. 30; Köhler, pp. 302 ff., 335, pl. 98a; Leitschuh, p. 242 f.

[2] Cf. the full-length figures of Rome and Constantinople on the diptych in Vienna: Delbrueck, no. 38.

[3] Boinet, pl. 114; Leitschuh, p. 245.

of God, appearing immediately over the emperor's crown, gives this picture an investiture-character; but this is not stressed, and the hand is treated rather as if it were a member of the imperial regalia like the crown itself, the orb, and the sceptre. The architecture, with its two tiers of columns and the looped-backed curtains, would seem to be derived from a western prototype of about 400.[1]

More ambitious compositions are found in the Vivian Bible, the Codex Aureus from St. Emmeram at Regensburg now in Munich, and in the Bible of San Callisto; the ruler-effigy is here expanded into a ceremonial composition, which in the Vivian Bible is conceived as a presentation-scene and an event of real life, but in the two later books as an imperial allegory. The picture of Abbot Vivian,[2] followed by his monks, presenting his bible to Charles the Bald, shows the emperor enthroned in the middle, between two courtiers in civil costume and two military attendants; he wears the Byzantine silk garments which he is known to have affected on Sundays and festal occasions.[3] The monks grouped in the foreground seem to be by no means awed into discipline and silence, but are chattering and gesticulating in a perfectly unconstrained way. There is none of the rigidity of oriental etiquette which marks the composition on the disk of Theodosius; the whole tone is delightfully natural and informal, and one is inclined to think that the artist must have been present

[1] Cf. Rodenwaldt in *NGG.* 1925, pp. 33 ff.
[2] Boinet, pl. 51.
[3] Ébersolt, *Orient et occident*, i. p. 60.

at the interview, presumably as one of the lively monks in the foreground. This conversion of a court-ceremony into a cheerful conversation-piece is a remarkable achievement; and there is very little doubt that it was an original invention of the Tours artist. Wegner has noted the resemblance between this scene and an *adlocutio* on the Column of Marcus Aurelius.[1] It might also be compared with the two pictures of Christ before Pilate in the Codex Rossanensis, where the disposition of the bystanders is very similar.[2] But in neither of these earlier attempts at group-composition do we find the same psychological unity as in the dedication-picture of the Vivian Bible. The use of gesture and the direction of the glance to create emotional continuity has been noted as a characteristic device of late medieval painting in Holland;[3] it is here found already developed six centuries earlier in Carolingian painting.

The imperial groups in the Munich Codex Aureus and the Bible of S. Callisto are more complex in idea and structure, though they have less human significance than the dedication-scene in the Vivian Bible. In the Codex Aureus (Staatsbibliothek cod. 14000, fol. 5vo),[4] Charles the Bald is enthroned under a magnificent domed baldacchino like that which spans the judgement-seat of Pilate in the Codex Rossanensis and appears many times in later Byzantine MSS. The hand of God over the emperor's

[1] *Op. cit.*, p. 109.
[2] Kömstedt, *Vormittelalterliche Malerei*, figs. 94-95.
[3] Pächt in *Kunstwissenschaftliche Forschungen*, ii. (1933), p. 94.
[4] Boinet, pl. 115.

head, as in the Paris Psalter, places this picture in the class of investiture-scenes; and the satellites are not simply court-officials, but ideal supporters of the imperial dignity. To right and left, between the pillars of the baldacchino, are the emperor's armour-bearers; and beyond them are female figures in mural crowns, with burgeoning cornucopias, who are designated by verses in the margin as Francia and Gotia. Above are two angels pointing down towards the emperor.

The frontispiece of the Bible of S. Callisto[1] belongs to the same type of representation, except that it inclines more to the satellite-group than to the investiture-group, in that the hand of God is absent and the accompanying personages are less abstract in character. The two armour-bearers to the left are more like ordinary soldiers, and the two women have discarded their mural crowns and horns of abundance. The ideal figures, like the four Virtues, who appear between the columns of the curious baldacchino-throne, and the two angels, are subordinate in importance and merely form a discreet group in the background. In both these pictures the emperor is very much larger than the attendants, and is quite unconcerned by their presence.

Apart from these explicit representations of Carolingian rulers, there are many other effigies of historic princes such as David and Herod which are really imperial-portraits in disguise. Among these we ought to distinguish two classes: those in which the artist, having to represent a king, arrays him in the likeness

[1] Boinet, pl. 121; Leitschuh, p. 248 f.

of his own sovereign because no other type of royal effigy is imaginable; and those which deliberately allude to a living ruler in the lineaments of a dead one. The distinction lies not so much in the picture as in the mind of the artist; and it would seem hardly worth mentioning were it not for the evident deliberateness of the allusion in the second case. Such effigies as the Herod in the Bible of S. Callisto[1] and the Pilate in the Milan Passion-diptych are, in fact, indistinguishable from Carolingian ruler-types, though, needless to say, the Carolingian artist intended no personal reference to his master. On the other hand, the David-portrait in Carolingian psalters evidently has such a reference. For example, in the British Museum Lothair Psalter, the full-page picture of the Psalmist is intentionally balanced against the full-page picture of the king;[2] and in the Vivian Bible the dedication-scene is balanced by a composition with David, with the actual features of Charles the Bald and wearing the Frankish crown, dancing and playing the harp, while his satellites Asap, Ethan, Heman, and Jeduthun accompany him on various instruments.[3] In the Golden Psalter at St. Gall the dancing attendants carry castanets and hold scarves over their heads in the antique manner;[4] and a similar motif is found in the Vatican MS. of Cosmas Indicopleustes, in the miniature which shows David and Solomon arrayed in Byzantine imperial dress.[5] The discovery of the type was, no doubt, easy enough. What interests

[1] Boinet, pl. 125a.
[2] Boinet, pl. 79.
[3] Boinet, pl. 49; cf. also the Psalter of Charles the Bald: Boinet, pl. 113a.
[4] Boinet, pl. 144a.
[5] Stornajolo, pl. 26.

us is rather the persistence of the David-motif in Carolingian art; this is probably to be explained by the fact that Charles the Great himself bore the nickname of David in the Alcuinian circle,[1] and that his successors liked to see themselves represented in this rôle.

The other large class of single figures in Carolingian art, apart from the Majestas, is the series of Evangelist-portraits in gospel-books and other MSS. and their counterparts in ivory-carving. There are two main divisions of the traditional Evangelist type in late-antique art, as distinguished by Friend: the standing and the seated, which he ascribes respectively to Alexandria and Asia Minor (Ephesus?).[2] The former type, of which early examples may be seen on the throne of Maximian and in the Vatican Cosmas MS., is of little importance to the student of Carolingian art, which adopted exclusively the seated type. This appears in several variant forms, derived from prototypes of different origins and dates. These may be divided into two main groups: *a*, that in which the Evangelist is placed in a landscape setting; and *b*, that in which he appears against an architectural background.

The Evangelist in a landscape is found in one of the earliest groups of Carolingian MSS., the so-called Schola Palatina, which includes the Gospel-book from the imperial Schatzkammer in Vienna,[3] and the gospels in the cathedral-treasury at Aachen,[4] in

[1] Laistner, *op. cit.*, p. 158.

[2] *Art Studies*, v. (1927), pp. 124, 134 ff.

[3] Boinet, pls. 58-9.

[4] Boinet, pl. 60a.

Brussels (from Xanten),[1] and in Berlin (from Cleve).[2] The Vienna MS. contains four miniatures of the Evangelists: white-robed figures, composing their works in a hillocky landscape. Except for the large gold haloes behind their heads, they are entirely antique in style. The proportions are natural, the gestures easy; the modelling of the bodies is coherent and assured, and the lighting of the scene is in accordance with antique conventions. There are no symbols: a sign of an early prototype. The border is adorned with a band of acanthus. The Berlin MS. follows the same scheme, except that the Evangelists now have their symbols, in accordance with the regular western practice, and that the plastic consistency shows signs of degenerating into a more linear style. In the Aachen manuscript the four Evangelists, with their symbols, occupy the same rocky ravine, which is seen from above in a kind of bird's-eye perspective; the border also is richer, and contains imitations of jewelled appliques. The sense of atmosphere and the intent to create an illusion are, however, still prominent. The Evangelists of the Brussels MS. are seated in a row in the foreground, with their symbols over their heads, and above them Christ enthroned on a globe. The individual figures are still handled in the plastic style, but their relation to the landscape—not to mention the landscape itself—has become much vaguer.

The Evangelists in the Schatzkammer Gospels come nearest to the ancient style: so near, indeed, that Goldschmidt[3] is inclined to think that the

[1] Boinet, pl. 60b. [2] Boinet, pl. 70. [3] *German Illumination*, i. p. 9 f.

painter may actually have been a Byzantine; he does not countenance the theory, however, that this was the *Demetrius Presbyter* whose name appears in gold rustic capitals on the margin of the miniature depicting St. Matthew. It seems more probable that the artist, trained perhaps in Italy, has shown unusual skill in copying a prototype of about 400.

The so-called Schola Palatina, to which these MSS. belong, is generally localised at Aachen. From there it was transplanted to Rheims, probably by Archbishop Ebo (816–35), who had been imperial librarian; the connexion is visible in the gospel-book, now at Épernay, which bears his name.[1] It is true that the easy, unconstrained style of the Vienna book and its colleagues has undergone a violent change. Whereas the Evangelists of the Schola Palatina were tranquil and absorbed in their work, their successors at Rheims behave as though possessed with a demon of self-consciousness: they are either furiously busy, or gaze wildly round; their clothes are all crumpled and awry, as though to signify their inner conflict and agony; and the landscape upheaves itself in sympathy. This orgiastic tempo, which also characterises the most famous product of this school, the Utrecht Psalter, calms down considerably in the later members of the group, such as the Gospels from Blois[2] and Loisel[3] in the Bibliothèque Nationale; but the type of outdoor Evangelist persists to the end. It reappears, like other Rheims features, in the MSS. of Tours; the

[1] Boinet, pls. 68–9.
[2] Boinet, pl. 72.
[3] Boinet, pl. 74.

Evangelists in the Moutier-Grandval and Vivian Bibles belong to this category, though the landscape becomes more and more attenuated. In Franco-Saxon MSS. like the Gospels of Francis II[1] the Evangelists are seated under markedly eastern-looking trees—palms and those peculiar mushroom-growths beloved of the artists of the Vienna Genesis.

The second type of Carolingian Evangelist-portrait—that with the architectural background[2]—also appears fully developed right from the beginning, and is also derived from late-antique prototypes, though of an altogether different order from the type of the Evangelist in a landscape. The earliest MS. of the Ada group, the Evangelistary written by Godescalc for Charles in 781–3,[3] contains a figure of Christ, Evangelist-portraits and a symbolical representation of the Fountain of Life. The Evangelists are seated at their desks, pen in hand, composing their Gospels. We recognise at once, in a somewhat different shape, the type of the Lindisfarne book, of the Canterbury Gospels at Cambridge, of the Codex Amiatinus; we recall the St. Mark with his Inspiration in the Codex Rossanensis, the Dioscorides illustrations, and the Poet and his Muse on the diptych at Monza; we compare the Carolingian Evangelists with their Byzantine counterparts in Stavronikita 43 and other gospel-books of the tenth and later centuries. The author is derived from the Hellenistic seated philosopher, unbearded, like the poet of the Monza diptych, in the Ada MS., or bearded in the Lorsch Gospels according

[1] Boinet, pls. 98–9.
[2] Friend in *Art Studies*, v. (1927), pp. 137 ff.
[3] Boinet, pls. 3–4.

to the usual Byzantine fashion. The niche in which he is seated comes from the stage-architecture of the Asianic theatre, as Friend has pointed out.

The general scheme in all the MSS. of this group is the same, and follows the lead set by the Godescalc book; the detail becomes more elaborate, however, and the handling generally more accomplished and naturalistic. In the Ada codex,[1] named after the putative sister of Charles the Great who commissioned it about 800, the Evangelists sit at work in arched recesses lined with pigeon-holes, with their symbols above their heads. In the Abbeville book,[2] believed to have been given by Charles the Great to Angilbert, abbot of Saint-Riquier (790–814), the Evangelists are very similar, but rather less contorted and more comfortably accommodated to their niches. The MS. from St. Médard at Soissons,[3] now in the Bibliothèque Nationale, is said to have been given to that monastery in 827 by Louis the Pious and his wife Judith, but is probably earlier in date; this shows particular inventiveness in the architectural accessories, but the Evangelists are of the regular type. The same may be said of the Harley Gospels[4] in the British Museum (Harl. 2788) and the codex[5] from Lorsch which is partly in the Vatican and partly in the Batthyány library at Alba Julia in Rumania.

Plate XIII

In the later offshoots of the Ada school the figure-style tends to become linearised and to lose its antique plasticity, though the architectural setting is more successfully reproduced. One of these MSS., the Gospels

[1] Boinet, pl. 8. [2] Boinet, pl. 10. [3] Boinet, pls. 21-2.
[4] Boinet, pl. 13. [5] Boinet, pl. 17.

XIII. ST. LUKE: MINIATURE FROM THE ADA GOSPELS
Trier, Stadtbibliothek.

from St. Martin at Mainz, now in the Landesbibliothek at Gotha,[1] is very hybrid in style, the Evangelists being partly derived from insular models and partly from models coloured and shaded in the late-antique manner.

It is convenient to describe as portraits these ruler-effigies and Evangelist-types, although they cannot be regarded as reliable likenesses of historical personages. And in a sense this practice is logically justified; owing to the medieval habit, noted at the beginning of this chapter, of merging the type in the individual, these imaginary portraits do at least correspond to a notion of a man which was not purely intellectual, like the Greek ideal type, but was based on actual observation of life. It is therefore legitimate to think of Carolingian portraits as likenesses of contemporaries sustaining historical rôles. As we have seen, David may well appear in the guise of Lothair or Charles the Bald *dressed as* David. This tendency towards impersonation will also explain the wide variety of types which the same character may assume at different times, the iconographic inconsistencies, and yet the ultimate conviction these manifold features can convey. It is as though we were watching a large number of different actors playing the same rôles. We do not ask them all to look alike; we merely ask them to look convincing.

The figure of Christ himself in Carolingian art generally appears in a narrative context, especially on ivories. This is due quite simply to the fact that narrative is more accessible to the western mind than ecstatic imagery and symbolism. The majority of Carolingian

[1] Goldschmidt, *German Illumination*, i. pls. 46-7.

representations are thus based on the western popular style of the fourth and fifth centuries, which in its turn may well have come from monastic sources in Palestine. On the other hand, the hieratic tradition which east Christian art created in the fifth and sixth centuries, and which the Byzantines developed to its highest pitch after the iconoclastic period, left certain traces on Carolingian iconography, though its real influence on western art begins with the Ottonian period. These traces are most visible in works of art which were designed for cultivated audiences. In the Moutier-Grandval and Vivian Bibles, for example, we find the hieratic type of Christ enthroned in the almond-shaped glory, or mandorla, which first appears in Christian art in the miniature of the Ascension in the Rabula Gospels.[1] The Christ as Pantokrator occurs on one leaf of the ivory diptych in Berlin, whose sacred subject reproduces the scheme of contemporary consular diptychs, with their perfectly mundane setting;[2] such a composition evidently provided the models for the book-covers now in the Vatican and the Victoria and Albert Museum, which once belonged to the Lorsch Gospels and are therefore affiliated to the Ada group.[3] The hieratic type of the Tours bibles is distinct from this imperial type; its earliest manifestations are in the sixth century.[4] Sometimes Christ is seated on a sphere instead of a throne, as in the apse-mosaic of San Vitale at Ravenna;[5]

[1] Kömstedt, *Vormittelalterliche Malerei*, fig. 112.

[2] Vöge, *Kat.* no. 2, pl. 2.

[3] Goldschmidt, i. 13-14.

[4] E.g. in the Monastery of S. Jeremias at Saqqara: Dalton, p. 287, fig. 175.

[5] Peirce and Tyler, *L'art byzantin*, ii. pl. 77.

this is occasionally combined in Carolingian art with the mandorla, and a curious 8-shaped complex is the result—as on an ivory now in Berlin[1] which Goldschmidt places in his Ada group. The standing type in the mandorla occurs chiefly in representations of the Transfiguration, as on the ivory in the Victoria and Albert Museum.[2] This hieratic type of the Transfiguration appears first in the sixth century—for example, in the church of the monastery of St. Catherine on Mount Sinai.[3] This is included here among single-figure representations only because the mandorla isolates Christ from the narrative scene; he plays no active part in it, except in a supra-real sense. Large single figures of sacred personages, apart from Evangelists, are exceedingly rare in Carolingian art. The Zacharias and John the Baptist on the Lorsch bookcover at South Kensington are taken straight from an east Christian original of about 500 in the style of the Berlin sacred diptych. The Archangel at Leipzig[4] is also probably derived from an original of the same school. Like the Virgin of the Lorsch cover he has a fluted nimbus, which is a feature of Ada style. But he has lost his antique stability and become much more ornamental; and the portrait-like irregularity of his face confirms the remarks made above on the subject of Carolingian impersonation.

Plate XIV opp. p. 146

The division of the subject-matter of Carolingian art into two groups, narrative and effigy, has been found to correspond roughly to a chronological division of the prototypes. The narrative themes

[1] Goldschmidt, i. 23.
[2] Goldschmidt, i. 69.
[3] Dalton, p. 384, fig. 225.
[4] Goldschmidt, i. 11.

derive, on the whole, from compositions invented between about 350 and 450, while the effigies are based on hieratic motifs which date from about 450–550. In other words, the models for the narrative themes are mainly western in form, if not in origin, and the models for the effigies are eastern. There remains, however, a third category of subject-matter to be dealt with: the allegory in all its forms, sacred and profane. Allegorical compositions are so important a feature of Carolingian art, as of western medieval art as a whole, and their origins are so little understood that they must be relegated to a separate chapter.

XIV. IVORY PANEL: CHRIST ENTHRONED
Berlin, Deutsches Museum.

III

THE allegorical character of medieval representational art in western Europe is familiar to every student of iconography.[1] What is less well understood is the history of the allegory as a form of artistic expression; and it is this aspect, rather than its content, that we must now consider. It is necessary, in the first place, to distinguish the allegory from the symbol, the personification, and the myth; and then to enquire when the allegorical representation, in its developed medieval shape, first made its appearance in European art.

With certain reservations it may be laid down that the allegory proper was not a means of expression very congenial to the antique imagination. When the Greeks wished to make an abstract notion accessible in concrete form, they either invented a personification to symbolise it explicitly or veiled its moral implications in a myth. Much more rarely they created a dramatic legend in which the personifications appeared in their own guise as actors. An early example of such a scene is the contest between Justice and Injustice on the chest of Cypselus, that Corinthian work of the sixth century B.C. which is known to us only from the description in Pausanias.[2] The famous

[1] Van Marle, *Iconographie de l'art profane au moyen-âge et à la renaissance*, ii.
[2] v. 17, 5—19, 10; for a detailed discussion and reconstruction, see von Massow in *AM.* xli. (1916), pp. 1 ff.

picture of Calumny by Apelles,[1] mentioned by Lucian and fancifully recreated by Botticelli and other masters of the Renascence, seems to have had something of the dramatic action necessary to the true allegory; but we can only guess how far this action depended on any continuous psychological characterisation, and how far the relation between the figures was simply mechanical and external. The second alternative seems rather the more probable when we examine the relief of the Apotheosis of Homer by Archelaus of Priene in the British Museum.[2] In this composition, which has the appearance of having been copied from a painting, a large series of mythological characters and personifications are arranged on a shelved mountain-side. They ostensibly pay tribute to the seated figure of Homer in the bottom left-hand corner; but actually the dramatic continuity of the scene is of the slightest, and this lack of unified action makes it doubtful whether this can properly be called a narrative allegory in the strictest sense. The same may be said of the frequent groups of personifications of cities and virtues on the reverse of Roman coins; these greetings have about as much intimate psychological value as the "cordial relations" between statesmen of rival powers.

It seems clear that when the ancients wished to suggest at all a complex or delicate series of moral ideas, they had recourse to myth. It has long since been recognised that the mythological scenes carved

[1] See Förster in the Prussian *Jahrbuch*, viii. (1887), pp. 29 ff., 89 ff; xv. (1894), pp. 27 ff.; cf. Pfuhl, *Malerei und Zeichnung der Griechen*, pp. 739, 743.

[2] 2191; see Bulle, *op. cit.*, pp. 333 ff.

on the front of Roman sarcophagi and painted on the ceilings and walls of Roman tombs are not merely decorative in intention, but contain allusions to the adventures of the soul in the after-life.[1] The influence of mystery-religions is here universally admitted; and this tendency of the oriental idea to embody itself in the material forms of European art is the most striking and complete illustration of the interpenetration of eastern and western thought in the Roman Empire. Here again, as has so often happened, the fecundation of the Hellenic body by the oriental spirit produced the specifically European phenomenon.

In addition, however, to this mystical recreation of ancient mythology in late antique pagan art,[2] a new tendency arises among Christian writers, and subsequently among Christian artists, to apply this allegorical technique to historical, and not merely to legendary events. Granted that the dividing line between history and myth was not so sharply drawn in antiquity as it is in modern times, the difference between the moralisation of an imaginary event and of a real one is still sufficiently marked to justify our treating them as separate processes. It seems probable, however, that the instinct to search for moral lessons in history is as much an oriental phenomenon as the corresponding attitude towards myth. It has been observed that the Jews, unlike the Greeks, had a theory of history;[3] the past, like the future, was

[1] Cf. Strong, *Apotheosis and After-Life*, esp. pp. 112 ff.

[2] Cf. Eisler, "Orphisch-dionysische Mysteriengedanken in der christlichen Antike" (*Vorträge der Bibliothek Warburg*, ii. (1922–3), pp. 159 ff.).

[3] Dawson in *A Monument to St. Augustine*, p. 45.

regulated by design, not subject to chance, and it was therefore natural to look behind cause and event for a moral purpose.

This attitude is already found as early as the first century in the Jewish writer, Philo of Alexandria,[1] who interpreted the characters in biblical history as good and bad dispositions of the soul. The Alexandrian theologians expanded this idea with enthusiasm; and we find Origen (185–253) enunciating the famous doctrine of the triple meaning of the scriptures—literal, moral, and mystical.[2] In these interpretations the literal meaning fared worst; and it is not surprising to observe the Fathers of the Church, Hilary, Ambrose, or Augustine, emphatically upholding the historical validity of holy writ. The medieval position was defined by Gregory the Great, who described the threefold meaning of biblical history as literal, doctrinal, and moral.[3]

The same notion of history is responsible for the concordance of events in the Old and New Testaments, which, as set out in the *Dittochaeon* of Prudentius, exercised its well-known effect on medieval iconography. It runs all through the encyclopaedic conception of human knowledge, as found in St. Isidore[4] and the Venerable Bede:[5] the Carolingian contribution to this stock being the *Glossa Ordinaria* of Walafrid Strabo, Abbot of Reichenau (809–43).[6]

[1] Bréhier, E., *Les idées philosophiques de Philon d'Alexandrie*, pp. 35 ff.

[2] *Contra Celsum*, iv. 15. For a discussion of Origen's exegetic principles, see Laistner, *op. cit.*, p. 43 f.

[3] *Ibid.*, p. 76. [4] *Ibid.*, p. 92 f. [5] *Ibid.*, p. 123. [6] *Ibid.*, p. 252.

It also explains why the Virtues and Vices acquired the status of independent characters, as they appear in the *Psychomachia* of Prudentius,[1] and ceased to be the lifeless abstractions they had been in pagan antiquity.

Combined with this moralising tendency we find the Neo-Pythagorean notion of the moral value of numbers; here again the influence of Philo is evident.[2] The sacred numbers seven and twelve are respectively the sum and the product of the number of the soul (four) and the number of the body (three). By sevens were reckoned the sacraments, the virtues, the ages of life, the wonders of the world, the liberal arts, and the days of the week; and by twelves the Prophets and Apostles and the months of the year. The numbers three and four, in addition, denoted the Persons of the Trinity, on the one hand, and the Evangelists, on the other.

This allegorical mode of expression appears, as far as we are concerned, in literature earlier than in the plastic arts. Apart from the *Psychomachia* of Prudentius, whose contribution to the iconography of medieval art is well known, it is only necessary to mention the *Marriage of Mercury and Philology* by Martianus Capella.[3] This curious composition provided the types of the seven liberal arts: Grammar, an awe-inspiring old woman with a birch; meagre Dialectic, concealing a snake in the folds of her black mantle; Rhetoric in breastplate and helmet;

[1] Stettiner, *Die illustrierten Prudentiushandschriften*, pp. 155 ff.

[2] Bréhier, *op. cit.*, p. 43.

[3] See van Marle, *Iconographie de l'art profane*, ii. pp. 204 ff., for the influence of Martianus Capella on medieval art.

Arithmetic counting on her fingers; Geometry holding a compass and sphere; Astronomy with her sextant; Music playing on a psaltery in the form of a golden buckler. This romance was composed in the fifth century, but whether it was illustrated at the same period we do not know. The earliest reference to a picture of the seven arts in which the influence of Martianus Capella is discernible seems to be in a poem by Theodulf of Orleans describing a mosaic in the palace at Aachen.[1] There was a globe from which grew a tree, bearing leaves and fruit and mounting upward to the stars. Grammar sat at its root, crowned, and with whip and sword in hand. Rhetoric and Dialectic sat on a branch to the right, and the Four Cardinal Virtues on a branch to the left. Arithmetic embraced the tree; Music and Geometry sat among the upper branches, with Astronomy on the middle stem, and Wisdom, Logic, Ethic, and Physic above. The influence of Martianus also appears in another poem by Theodulf which describes separate figures of the seven arts.[2] Another allegorical picture recorded by the same poet represented Amphitrite encircling the world, in the middle of which was Cybele, with a boy at her breast, a mural crown on her head, a snake in her bosom, and in her hands a key, cymbals, and weapons. Near by stood a fruit-basket; and in front were hens, sheep, tamed lions, and an empty chariot.[3] It is hard to believe that such compositions —if, indeed, they ever existed and were not figments

[1] *PLAC.* i. p. 544; Schlosser, 1026.
[2] *PLAC.* i. p. 629; Schlosser, 1028.
[3] *PLAC.* i. p. 548; Schlosser, 1031.

of the poetical imagination[1]—were invented in the ninth century; they may have been actual late-antique works brought from Rome, Ravenna, or Constantinople, or at least copies of such prototypes. It is recorded that Charles possessed a table with a plan of Constantinople on the top;[2] and it is not inconceivable that he may also have owned a Byzantine allegorical composition something like the tapestry of Hestia Polyolbos, surrounded by cupids carrying medallions inscribed with the words *Good Luck*, *Prosperity*, etc., which is now in the Bliss collection.[3] We can get some idea of the appearance of the figures described by Theodulf from the Music, Arithmetic, Geometry, and Astrology in the Boethius codex at Bamberg,[4] a Tours MS. dating from about 850; from the Francia and the Gotia with their mural crowns and horns of abundance in the Munich Codex Aureus;[5] and from the four Virtues in the Vivian Bible.[6]

Mythological motifs, which may or may not have an allegorical meaning, appear in manuscripts of the Tours school, especially as marginal vignettes. For example, Bellerophon and the Chimaera, and a Centaur shooting a deer, griffins, and other classical monsters are found in the Vivian Bible and the Lothair gospels; antique javelin-throwers with shields in the Blois MS.; and Tritons blowing horns in the

[1] For this question, cf. the discussion on the *Imagines* of Philostratus between Friederichs, *Die philostratischen Bilder*, and Brunn in *Jahrb. f. Philologie*, ciii. (1871), pp. 1 ff., 81 ff.

[2] Schlosser, 1032; Einhard, *Vita*, ch. 33.

[3] Volbach-Salles-Duthuit, *Art byzantin*, pls. 83-4; Peirce and Tyler, *L'art byzantin*, i. pls. 153-4.

[4] Boinet, pl. 57b; Köhler, pl. 90.

[5] Boinet, pl. 115.

[6] Boinet, pl. 49; Köhler, pl. 72.

gospels of Loisel. More explicitly allegorised personifications of the Sun and Moon, Earth and Ocean, Church and Synagogue, are regular accompaniments to the Crucifixion on Metz ivories; and convert what would otherwise be a narrative picture into a symbolic representation of the Redemption. The Libri Carolini had spoken decidedly on the undesirability of reproducing such heathen legends and stories.[1] River-gods and earth-gods were to be avoided; likewise the sun and moon, months and seasons, and naked or semi-naked figures generally—Vulcan, Scylla, the Sirens, Bellerophon and the Chimaera, and other hybrid monsters such as the Centaur and the Minotaur. But these injunctions were generally disregarded.[2] The ancient tradition was too strong; and the medieval habit of finding moral justifications for stories which it could not bear to discard doubtless permitted the irregularity to continue unheeded.

In so far as medieval allegory depended on antique notions it operated by means of personifications and motifs derived from classical mythology.[3] These were

[1] iii. 23; see Leitschuh, pp. 32 ff.

[2] Explicit illustrations to Virgil's Eclogues appear on the handle of a liturgical fan (Tours: *c.* 850) now in the Bargello at Florence (Goldschmidt, i. 155 ; cf. also the fabulous monsters in scrolls on two panels in the Musée de Cluny (Goldschmidt, i. 156-7), which may have been influenced by a Byzantine or Sasanian silk textile, like the earlier Anglo-Saxon version of the same theme (*c.* 700) on the Easby cross-shaft in the Victoria and Albert Museum (Collingwood, *Northumbrian Crosses*, fig. 53).

[3] For a curious mixture of biblical and mythological motifs in one scene, see the ivory-carving (Tours: *c.* 850, on the back of a Byzantine diptych panel of 506) now in the Louvre (Goldschmidt, i. 158); Adam and Eve in the Garden of Eden are accompanied not only by the usual beasts, but also by centaurs, satyrs, sirens, griffins, etc. The influence of the Physiologus, or Alexandrian bestiary, is probable; see Woodruff on the Berne MS. of the Physiologus in *Art Bulletin*, xii. (1930), pp. 226 ff.

not, however, the only devices for giving abstract ideas a tangible shape. The earliest Christian art, for reasons already given, veiled its beliefs behind symbols of non-human shape, such as the fish, the lamb, and the peacock. Even after the creation of a Christian figure-art these symbols still retained a certain value as shorthand compendia; and in the iconoclastic period, as is well known, they regained their full significance. In the west they were not so popular; the comparatively straightforward, rationalistic, and practical minds of the Frankish theologians had less use for these mystical fetishes than their Byzantine brethren, who were more continuously exposed to the influence of religions like Mazdaism and Islam and their artistic anthropophobia.[1] It happens, however, that Carolingian art derived from the east certain of these non-human symbolic motifs; and they have thus become an integral part of the western pictorial tradition.

The most conspicuous of these is the Fountain of Life.[2] It appears in all the gospel-books of the Ada group, as well as in the Armenian gospels at Etchmiadzin, and must also have appeared in their sixth-century prototype. The symbolism is undoubtedly oriental, but in this form has assumed a Hellenistic dress. The essential feature is the circular columned shrine, or *tempietto*, with a conical roof. Such buildings can be traced back at least as far as the first century B.C., where they occur on wall-paintings in the Villa

[1] See Strzygowski, *Origin of Christian Church Art*, pp. 102 ff.

[2] Underhill in *Burl. Mag.* xvii (1910), pp. 99 ff., for the history of this motif; cf. Soulier, *Influences orientales dans la peinture toscane*, p. 39. See also Leitschuh, pp. 254 ff. Cf. Paulinus of Nola (Migne lxi. col. 337).

of Diomede at Pompeii [1] and in the house at Boscoreale whose decorations are now in New York.[2] *Tholoi*, or rotundas, are mentioned by Vitruvius [3] among the architectural features painted by Apaturius of Alabanda in the small assembly hall at Tralles in Asia Minor; and similar structures stand between projecting wings in the rock-cut façades of Petra.[4] In later times the motif is seen in the mosaics of St. George at Salonica [5] and in the great mosque of Damascus; [6] and in its specialised use as a fountain became the regular type for such buildings in Byzantine and Islamic architecture. The connexion of this motif with stage-scenery, assured in the case of Apaturius and presumed in the case of the dome-mosaics at Salonica, suggests the origin of another remarkable piece of symbolic architecture, the frontispiece from *Plate XV* the Gospels of St. Médard from Soissons, now in the Bibliothèque Nationale (MS. lat. 8850, fol. 1vo).[7] This remarkable composition is in three parts: the colonnade on the ground floor with the divided curtain; the row of medallions containing the symbols of the Evangelists; and the Apocalyptic scene at the top—apparently an excerpt from a framed miniature—with the twenty-four Elders adoring the Lamb. This composition is plainly not a straightforward illustration of the fourth chapter of the Book of Revelation, but its allegorical significance is not clear; the colonnade, in particular, with its *scaenae frons*

[1] Curtius, *Die Wandmalerei Pompejis*, fig. 76.
[2] *Ibid.*, fig. 72. [3] vii. 5. [4] Kennedy, *Petra*, fig. 114.
[5] Diehl—Le Tourneau—Saladin, *Salonique*, pl. ii. 2.
[6] Creswell, *Early Muslim Architecture*, pl. 44.
[7] Boinet, pl. 18a. See Leitschuh, p. 258 f.

XV. FRONTISPIECE TO THE GOSPELS OF SAINT-MEDARD-DE-SOISSONS
Paris, Bibliothèque Nationale.

derived from antique stage-architecture, being hard to explain. Leitschuh[1] believes it to be an allegory of the church, and thinks it may be based on a confused recollection of the interior of the palace-church at Aachen, which seems to have had Apocalyptic representations in the dome. It is also conceivable that the three zones correspond to the three aspects of the Deity referred to in the text inscribed between the columns: *Sanctus Sanctus Sanctus Dominus Deus Omnipotens Qui erat Et qui est Et qui uenturus est* (Rev. iv. 8). If this is understood as referring to the Old Testament, the New Testament, and the Second Coming, the church at Aachen would symbolise the temple of Solomon, in accordance with the regular Carolingian convention,[2] the Evangelists' symbols the New Testament, and the Adoration of the Lamb the Second Coming. It is uncertain whether this three-storeyed edifice existed in the sixth-century prototype, or was invented by the Carolingian artist. As it is unique, whereas the Fountain of Life, the Evangelist-portraits, and the arcaded canon-tables recur in all the MSS. of this group, it seems more probable that it was a Carolingian addition; the very mixed spatial system, with the closed scene below, the open one above, and both combined in the middle, also makes it unlikely as a specimen of sixth-century design.

An allegorical intention is also detectable in a pair of tall, narrow ivory panels which must once have adorned the covers of a sacramentary, and which are now divided between the Fitzwilliam Museum at

[1] *Op. cit.*, p. 260.

[2] See Buchner, *Einhards Künstler- und Gelehrtenleben*, pp. 69 ff.

Plate XVI opp. p. 166

Cambridge and the Stadtbibliothek at Frankfort.[1] On each panel is an archbishop in a pallium, surrounded by singing deacons. It is probable that the officiating priest is a likeness of the ecclesiastic who commissioned the sacramentary; but the figures are not so much portraits of a specific person as a symbolic representation of the liturgy itself. This is not illustrated in a detailed sequence of sacramental acts, as on the covers of the Drogo Sacramentary, but in two comprehensive moments which embrace the whole mystery. On the Cambridge panel the priest stands with right hand raised in blessing and the left holding open a book at the first words of the twenty-fourth psalm; on the Frankfort panel he stands before an altar at the beginning of the mass. In this way the two aspects of the priest as sacrificant and spiritual father are symbolically expressed.

This practice of overlaying one meaning upon another—the mystical upon the doctrinal, and the doctrinal upon the literal—is only gradually developed. In the art of the fourth century they are still distinct; in the fifth the doctrinal allusion is combined with the literal narrative; and in the sixth the mystical element is elaborated. All these have interpenetrated by the ninth century, under the pressure of encyclopaedic thought imposed by Gregory, Isidore, and Bede. The allegorical inventions of the ninth century, like the architectural frontispiece of the Gospels of St. Médard and the liturgical ivories at Cambridge and Frankfort, are concerned not with the history of an

[1] Goldschmidt, i. 120-21; the panel of St. Gregory at Heiligenkreuz (G. i. 122) is by the same artist (*c.* 900).

institution, but with its mystical reality as here present. This projection of the spiritual life of the Church into the foreground of time, which was somewhat obscured by the archaising methods of early Carolingian art, now becomes a conspicuous feature of the religious art of western Europe; and it is in these allegories that we first recognise its significance.

PART THREE

THE FORM AND STRUCTURE OF CAROLINGIAN ART

I

THE fundamental problem of all representational art is to discover a formula by which the three dimensions of the real world can be converted into the two dimensions of the ideal world of the picture. This problem has been solved in a scientific and systematic manner only once: by the invention of vanishing-point perspective in Florence at the beginning of the fifteenth century.[1] It is therefore useless to expect to find a complete mastery of the space-surface metaphor at any previous date; the issue is evaded by all oriental art, which contents itself with an arbitrary, though intelligible, approximation, and in the art of all savage peoples and primitive civilisations of every period. Only the Greeks and Romans attempted frankly to face the problem, and even they only arrived at a tentative and partial solution;[2] as, however, their efforts affected Carolingian and Byzantine painting, and consequently all medieval art, to an appreciable extent, it seems necessary to give some account of antique methods of representing the solid world on a flat surface.

[1] For this subject in all its aspects, see Panofsky in *Vorträge der Bibliothek Warburg*, 1924–5, pp. 258 ff.

[2] Panofsky, pp. 265 ff.

Primitive art is nominalist in its attitude to the objects it has to represent. Men, animals, trees, and all other subject-matter are units which are outlined in their most characteristic shape upon a neutral ground. Their relation to each other, if any, is psychological, not aesthetic; and their relation to their context is ignored altogether. These units are placed paratactically all over the surface to be decorated. Space, as we understand it, does not exist; and at first even the surface is not subdivided or otherwise organised. Subsequently this is cut up into strips, or friezes; and these are further partitioned into panels. The rectangular frame thus created marks the first stage in the isolation of a tract of space in which certain figures with a common interest are enclosed, and by which they may be measured and interrelated; but this process is a long and difficult one. Though the figures now occupy a little plot of their own, their movements are still rigidly circumscribed; they can only be shifted sideways or up and down, but not inwards or outwards, and they remain paper-thin silhouettes, pressed, as it were, between two sheets of glass. Their gradual release may be studied on Attic vase-paintings from about 550 to 450 B.C. The first concession to depth is overlapping; the next is the front-view of things previously thought of in profile, such as chariots and horses; finally we come to foreshortening and the oblique view of faces, buildings, wheels, and so forth.[1] The representation of objects standing

[1] The Greek word is *κατάγραφα*, which Pliny, who renders it by *obliquae imagines* (*NH*. xxxv. 56), ascribes to Cimon of Cleonae (*c*. 530 B.C.?): see Holwerda in *JdI*. v. (1890), p. 258.

free in space has really begun; figures are separated from their background and are allowed a limited, but perceptible movement in the imaginary third dimension.

This admission that space exists for pictorial purposes entails a certain responsibility with regard to the background against which the figures stand out. It is no longer enough to differentiate figure and ground as "being" and "not-being".[1] In relief-sculpture this continues down to the Hellenistic period, but there is reason to think that the great painters of the fourth century devoted their attention to the question of articulating the previously neutral ground. Even as early as the middle of the fifth century[2] inequalities of landscape are suggested by placing the figures on different levels, and by partly concealing the lower parts of some by means of rocks and folds in the earth. This invention may perhaps have been suggested by theatrical scenery; at any rate, it will be convenient to call the contrivance a "*coulisse*-landscape", since derivatives and elaborations of this type occur throughout the period that concerns us. At first these *coulisses* occur under and between the figures; but later, probably in Hellenistic art, they seem to have been enlarged and grouped so as to fill the whole background. The paintings so composed have disappeared; but their arrangement is probably reflected in the Telephus frieze from Pergamon[3] and in the Apotheosis of Homer relief in the British

[1] Cf. Panofsky, p. 271.

[2] Cf. the Niobid krater from Orvieto in the Louvre: Furtwängler-Reichhold, *Griechische Vasenmalerei*, pl. 108; Löwy, *Polygnot*, pp. 15 ff.

[3] *Altertümer von Pergamon*, iii. 2, pls. 31-2.

Museum.[1] Both these works, it will be observed, come from Asia Minor; and it is not unlikely that the extended use of the *coulisse*-landscape, which may be seen in many mythological compositions from Pompeii, was a development of the Pergamene and other Asiatic schools.

Architectural backgrounds were also a product of the Hellenistic age. In their simplest form, consisting of screen-walls placed immediately behind the actors, they are seen in the Niobe picture in Naples[2] which is thought to reproduce an original of the fourth century; in the mosaics by Dioscurides of Samos; and in many Pompeian paintings which are evidently adapted from older models. A genuine closed interior is found on the painted gravestone of Hediste from Pagasae in Thessaly;[3] and complete views of town-streets adorned the villa at Boscoreale.[4] The piled-up houses suggest a town on a hilly site, such as Priene; and this confirms the current opinion that these prospects are derived from scene-painting like that of Apaturius of Alabanda, and were not invented in Campania.

In all these examples the architecture is in the immediate foreground, and the space it encloses is comparatively shallow; the influence of theatrical scenery,[5]

[1] *BM. Cat. of Sculpture*, 2191.

[2] Rizzo, *Pittura ellenistico-romana*, pl. 88.

[3] Rizzo, *op. cit.*, pl. 48. [4] Rizzo, *op. cit.*, pl. 7.

[5] Panofsky, *op. cit.*, p. 308: he compares the evolution of space in painting with the evolution of the ancient stage from a plastic building, through the intermediate phase of relief-façade, to the hollow space which embraces actors and spectators alike; for examples of the three phases, cf. the theatre of Dionysus at Athens (fifth cent.), the theatre at Priene (rebuilt in the second cent.), and the theatre at Aspendus (*c.* A.D. 150).

which we should suspect even without the direct evidence of the comedy-scenes by Dioscurides of Samos and the literary testimony of Vitruvius about the work of Apaturius, appears to be decisive in Asia Minor and Greece down to the first century B.C. A very different type of architecture appears in the Pompeian picture of Medea and the daughters of Pelias;[1] the buildings are extremely attenuated and transparent, and there are wide spaces of foreground and sky. This scene comes from a decoration in the third style, and is thus to be derived in all probability from Alexandria. The palace of Circe in the Vatican Odyssey landscapes is of the same type;[2] and we may therefore guess that the inspiration of these wide aerial vistas ending in a great expanse of sea and sky is also Alexandria. A kindred view of nature appears in those Egyptising landscape-panels with crocodiles, pygmies, and other Nilotic features;[3] and the internal evidence for ascribing the whole class to Egypt is convincing, so long as we bear in mind that no single painting in this style has ever been found in that country. The character of the landscape, with its white buildings and hazy sub-tropical light, are, however, as appropriate to Alexandria as the broken, rocky ground and piled-up houses are to Asia Minor.

The native Roman taste appears in the garden-fresco at Prima Porta and in those dry, exact little views of villas[4] and harbours which may well reproduce the landscapes of the Augustan Ludius, or

[1] Curtius, pp. 293 ff., fig. 170. [2] Rizzo, pl. 162.
[3] See Rostovtsev in *RM.* xxvi. (1911), pp. 26 ff.
[4] Rostovtsev in *JdI.* xix. (1904), pp. 103 ff.

Studius, of whom Pliny records that he "introduced a delightful style of decorating walls with representations of villas, harbours, landscape-gardens, sacred groves, woods, hills, fishponds, straits, streams, and shores: any scene, in short, that took the fancy".[1]

This statement of Pliny's would seem to indicate that no hard and fast line can be drawn between the Egyptising tradition and the realistic Roman topographical style brought into fashion by Studius; and for this reason it is impossible to decide, when examining late-Roman book-paintings like the Vatican Virgil, whether to call their landscape style eastern or western. It is evident that there is no essential difference between the bird's-eye views of towns in the Virgil and in the Vatican MS. of Cosmas, a book which is naturally ascribed to Alexandria. On the other hand, there is a real distinction between these landscapes with a high horizon and a wide expanse and the *coulisse*-landscapes with their more normal viewpoint, but less extensive depth, and if it is necessary to make regional distinctions, we may provisionally call the first, or bird's-eye, landscape Roman-Alexandrian, and the second, or *coulisse*, landscape Asianic. Both survive in late-antique, and therefore in Carolingian art; and for this reason it has seemed desirable to insist at some length on their differences. This is also the justification for distinguishing as sharply as possible their derivatives in Carolingian book-painting and ivory-carving; although it must be remembered that as the artists of the ninth century drew quite uncritically upon models of varying dates

[1] *NH.* xxxv. 116 (trans. Jex-Blake and Sellers, p. 147).

a.

b.

XVI. IVORY PANELS WITH LITURGICAL SCENES
a. Cambridge, Fitzwilliam Museum.

b. Frankfurt, Stadtbibliothek.

and mutually incompatible styles, it is not surprising to find divergent methods of composition employed indiscriminately in the same book, and sometimes even in the same painting or carving.

The classical relief with a plain negative background, which was made continuously down to the middle of the second century A.D., gave way in the Antonine period, as we have seen, to the baroque relief in which the background disappears into a cave of shadow; in the second half of the fourth century it was artificially revived, especially in ivory-carvings,[1] and in the fifth century it was used in Ravennate sarcophagi, though with a somewhat different intention.[2] The only Carolingian works where it occurs are ivory-carvings copied from western models of about A.D. 400, such as the tall panel subdivided into three scenes, now in the British Museum.[3] In book-painting the type is even rarer, since backgrounds of an architectural or landscape form are almost invariable in late-antique miniatures; examples may be found in the B. M. Lothair Psalter,[4] where the ruler-portrait and the figures of David and St. Jerome appear to descend from an original more or less in the manner of the Juliana Anicia of the Vienna Dioscorides. The figures of Boethius and Symmachus[5] in the Bamberg MS. are also isolated against a neutral ground. It is perhaps

[1] E.g. on the Brescia box (Kollwitz, *Die Lipsanothek von Brescia*, p. 41), and the "Provençal" group (see p. 54 f.).

[2] Riegl, *op. cit.*, pp. 188 ff.

[3] Dalton, *Cat.* no. 42; Goldschmidt, i. 24. For the style of the original, a five-part diptych, cf. the panels in Berlin and Paris (together: Volbach-Salles-Duthuit, pl. 10).

[4] Boinet, pls. 79–80.

[5] Boinet, pl. 57.

no accident that all these examples are portraits; the same convention applies in ancient portrait-painting, both at Pompeii and in the Fayum; and Grüneisen[1] suggests that this plain ground, which is generally blue, symbolises the spirit-world and indicates that the portrait was posthumous. This allusion would presumably have been forgotten in the Carolingian period, but the conventional tint survived.

The closed architectural setting is the regular accompaniment of the Evangelist-portraits in MSS. of the Ada group. It varies considerably in elaboration, from a simple crenellated wall in the Godescalc Gospels to niches of different shapes—rectangular, semicircular, etc.—in the later books like the Ada Gospels, the Abbeville Gospels, the Harley Gospels, and the Gospels of St. Médard de Soissons. The success with which the artist places his figure in its niche seems to depend upon the skill with which he imitates his late-antique model; there are no signs that he has any independent views on the perspectival rendering of space, beyond a general notion that retreating lines converge downwards if above the eye-line, and upwards if below. His mistakes and difficulties prove, however, that he was more attracted by the richness of the ornamental effect when copying all those cornices, curtains, pigeon-holes, desks, thrones, and other accessories, than genuinely interested in the problem of rendering three dimensions in two. The superior technical accomplishment of the antique perspectival scene is naively admitted by the northern artist, whose mind was, however,

[1] *Le portrait*, p. 38; cf. Wickhoff-Hartel, *Wiener Genesis*, p. 49 f.

irredeemably two-dimensional. Some progress is made, nevertheless. Panofsky compares the renderings of the Fountain of Life in the Godescalc and Soissons Gospels respectively.[1] In the earlier MS. (781–3) the circular building has a curved cornice but a flat base-line, like the corresponding rotunda in the Etchmiadzin Gospels; in the later MS. (*c.* 814 or *c.* 827), the surface of the water, which is below the eye-line, is shown with almost excessive extension.[2]

Almost the only Carolingian miniature in which an interior is adequately shown is the Exodus picture in the Moutier-Grandval Bible;[3] the converging lines of the coffered ceiling are as conscientiously managed as in the Death of Dido in the Vatican Virgil,[4] a resemblance which alone makes it certain that the prototype of this miniature in the Tours MS. was a Latin original of the fifth century. Otherwise it is seldom clear whether the action of any given scene is taking place indoors or out of doors. The theatrical background of ancient painting is doubtless responsible for this ambiguity; when an audience sat in the open air watching scenes, supposedly happening indoors, played against a screen in a sort of loggia, the resulting mental confusion can be imagined and excused. If the screen is large enough to fill the whole picture space, we can give it the benefit of the doubt, and assume that the architecture encloses ourselves

[1] *Op. cit.*, p. 310 f. and figs. 11 and 13.
[2] Cf. Panofsky, fig. 10.
[3] Boinet, pl. 44; cf. Panofsky, fig. 15.
[4] Kömstedt, *Vormittelalterliche Malerei*, fig. 32; Riegl, *Spätrömische Kunstindustrie* [2], p. 259 f., fig. 66.

also, as in a modern interior. But it not infrequently happens that these screens do not fill the space, and are seen to be mere *exedrae* in an open landscape: for example, in two of the Evangelist-pictures in the Schatzkammer Gospels[1] and in the pictures of SS. Matthew and Mark in the Munich Codex Aureus.[2]

It is noticeable, moreover, that in miniatures where the action, on the whole, takes place out of doors, certain episodes are made to happen either in front of a building or under a transparent baldacchino with only a roof supported by pillars, but no walls. These subterfuges recall the *ekkyklema* of the ancient theatre, that rolling platform which emerged on to the proscenium in order to disclose to the audience episodes which were supposed to take place behind the scenes. It is possible that when the death of Creon's daughter is displayed on the Munich Medea vase[3] as happening on a raised platform under a baldacchino, this is an actual reproduction of a scene in a tragedy. In any case, the baldacchino as the symbolic abbreviation of a palace had a long life in the history of European painting,[4] for it disappeared only in the fifteenth century, after the discovery of vanishing-point perspective made the adequate representation of interiors an easy matter.

In depicting scenes which avowedly take place in

[1] Boinet, pl. 59. [2] Boinet, pl. 118.

[3] Séchan, *Études sur la tragédie grecque*, p. 559.

[4] The baldacchino with the domed roof supported on pendentives occurs first in the Vienna Genesis (fol. iiii. 7: Wickhoff-Hartel, pl. 7). It is copied in Carolingian MSS.: Munich Codex Aureus (Boinet, pl. 115); Bible of S. Callisto (Boinet, pl. 125). As a symbol for a building, it confirms Sedlmayr's analysis of Justinianic architecture as a baldacchino-system: see *Kunstwissenschaftliche Forschungen*, ii. (1933), pp. 38 ff.

the open air, Carolingian artists make use of both the landscape-conventions of antique painting, the *coulisse* and the bird's-eye view. The first is the commoner, occurring in the Evangelist-pictures of the Schatzkammer Gospels and the other members of the Schola Palatina, and hence in the MSS. of the Rheims school, such as the Utrecht Psalter and the Épernay Gospels; and echoes of the same tradition are perceptible in the Tours MSS. which show the influence of Rheims, and later in the productions of the school of Saint-Denis. This arrangement of figures was less appropriate to ivories, though there are suggestions of the *coulisse* in the rocky ground-lines which separate the figures on different planes in carvings of the Liuthard group, such as the panel on the cover of the Paris Psalter of Charles the Bald[1] and the somewhat later panel, now at Zürich,[2] which illustrates Psalm xxvi. and therefore presumably also decorated the cover of a psalter. A curious extension of the *coulisse*-principle, not for landscape but for the separation of two figure-planes, is seen on the panel of the liturgical diptych at Cambridge,[3] where fluted semicircles, derived from the conch-shells behind the heads of the consuls on early sixth-century diptychs, are wedged quite arbitrarily between the priest and the deacons and again between them and the background. The same device is adopted, with clouds for *coulisses*, in the miniature representing the hierarchy of angels, apostles, martyrs, confessors, widows, and virgins in the Sacramentary from Metz in Paris.[4]

[1] Goldschmidt, i. 40a.
[2] Goldschmidt, i. 42.
[3] Goldschmidt, i. 120.
[4] Boinet, pl. 133.

The *coulisses* themselves are treated rather differently in the Carolingian copy and the late-antique model. In ancient art the crest is indeed the most important part and carries the strongest light, but the sloping sides are always conscientiously rendered even down to their roots in the deepest shadow; and this plastic conception of the whole is always respected in Byzantine art, so that the soft and billowy Hellenistic *coulisse* is converted into the unit like a tree-trunk sawn obliquely across which survives in Italian painting down to the beginning of the fifteenth century.[1] In Carolingian art, however, only the crest is given and the slopes leading up to it are left to the imagination; this explains why it is possible in Carolingian ivories to reduce the landscape-*coulisse* to a mere strip of knobbly bole-like matter, which gives the impression of having been squeezed out of a tube on to the surface of the ivory like paint on to a palette. Exactly the same indication of the crest of the *coulisse* without its flanks is adopted by the Persian miniaturists[2] and also by Chinese landscape-painters;[3] and from Carolingian painting the convention becomes customary in western miniatures of the Romanesque and Gothic periods. In later Carolingian MSS., such as the Golden Psalter of St. Gall,[4] the original function of the *coulisse* is forgotten; and instead of dividing one range of figures from another, it becomes a merely ornamental scalloped ground-line, and the figures trip along the crests of its furrows.

[1] Cf. Kallab in Vienna *Jahrbuch*, xxi. (1900), pp. 1 ff.
[2] Cf. Arménag Bey Sakisian, *La miniature persane*, pls. 52-3, etc.
[3] Cf. Sirén, *History of Early Chinese Painting*, i. pp. 121 ff.; ii. pp. 134 ff.
[4] Boinet, pl. 145.

The bird's-eye view was apparently less useful to Carolingian artists, presumably because it was seldom adopted in the late-antique models they copied. It occurs in the scenes with the history of St. Paul and St. Jerome in the Vivian Bible;[1] the resemblance between these landscapes, with their ships and harbours and walled cities, and miniatures in the Vatican Virgil and other western MSS. of the fifth century has already been noted. The most valuable feature of this system of composition to the Carolingian miniaturist was not so much the distant prospect of horizon and sky as the conventional representation of a town as a polygonal walled enclosure seen almost as a plan, and filled with either buildings or people, the latter being shown disproportionately large.

This town-symbol has a long previous history. On a Pompeian painting in the British Museum[2] representing the fall of Icarus, a walled city containing an amphitheatre floats like an apparition in the sky; in spite of its position at the top of the picture, it is seen steeply from above, although the temple on the headland in the foreground is seen from the "normal" point of view. Such an inconsistency would hardly have been permitted, no doubt, by the best Roman painters of the period; but that even a provincial Campanian decorator should have allowed himself such a perspectival absurdity in the first century A.D. shows that what we regard as spatial consistency had a very precarious hold over the antique pictorial

[1] Cf. the same subject in the Bible of S. Callisto: Boinet, pl. 122.

[2] *BM. Cat. of Paintings and Mosaics*, no. 28, pl. xii. A similar city appears in the Naples version of the same subject: Rizzo, pl. 167.

imagination. The well-known disproportion between human figures and buildings on the Column of Trajan becomes intelligible enough when we remember that it is essentially a work of popular art, in which Hellenistic conventions of space-representation are generally ignored; when we look, for example, at the view of the Roman camp in the background of the embassy-scene at the end of the first Dacian war,[1] we realise that the attempt at a systematic conception of space, which we noted in the paintings from the Boscoreale villa, has been abandoned, apparently without a struggle. The purely conceptual relationship of people to buildings and buildings to landscape was destined to last for more than a thousand years. Traces of the Hellenistic system—if so tentative an arrangement deserves the name—naturally persist in late-antique painting; the rationality of the architecture even in a work so late as the Joshua rotulus has led certain students to conjecture that it must have been based on an original painted before A.D. 300.[2] But this is not a necessary assumption; the decisive factor is always what we called the social factor—the taste of the patron. The prevailing taste in late-antique art is popular and non-Hellenistic; hence the ease with which irrational motifs like the bird's-eye view of a town find acceptance even in works of official art.

The immediate antecedents of the town-symbol in Carolingian art are so plentiful that we can hardly decide which exercised the greatest influence. The

[1] Lehmann-Hartleben, *Die Trajanssäule*, pl. 46, sec. c.
[2] E.g. Roosval, *Fornkristen Konst*, p. 5, fig. 3.

polygonal enclosure with towers at the angles occurs in the Vienna Genesis, both in the work of the miniaturists and the illusionists;[1] and is therefore current in Anatolia.[2] It appears in the Vatican Cosmas MS.,[3] and was therefore current at Alexandria. And as we have said, it is common in Latin MSS.[4] This is not, however, the only tradition of architectural representation in late-antique art; the naturalistic style of the Boscoreale villa survives, not only in the Joshua rotulus, but in the landscapes of the *coulisse*-type in archaising Byzantine MSS. like the Paris Psalter 139. There is a tendency, especially among French writers, to call this type of landscape Alexandrian.[5] This is quite unjustified. We have already shown that the geographical character of this style is appropriate to Greece and Asia Minor, not to Egypt; the buildings likewise have nothing Alexandrian about them, being derived from the regular colonnaded structures of the normal Hellenistic style of Asia Minor. In a manuscript, therefore, like the Utrecht Psalter there are no distinctively Alexandrian features; the polygonal walled towns might, indeed, be found in an Alexandrian MS., but, as we have seen, they are common to all late-antique styles of book-painting, and in this case belong to the fifth-century Latin prototype, whereas the colonnaded buildings, rotundas, sacred enclosures,

[1] Wickhoff-Hartel, pls. 9, 12, 13, 25, 27 (miniaturist); 38, 39 (illusionist).

[2] Cf. also the Sinope fragment (Kömstedt, fig. 83) and the Rossanensis (*id.* fig. 89).

[3] Stornajolo, pl. 48.

[4] Also on Roman mosaics: see the cities of Rome and Jerusalem on the triumphal arch of S. Maria Maggiore (Kömstedt, fig. 48).

[5] E.g. Diehl, *La peinture byzantine*, p. 44.

exedrae, etc., derive from the Asianic tradition like the *coulisse*-landscape in which they are set.

The mixture of the *coulisse*-landscape with the bird's-eye view of towns is not a Carolingian innovation; it is already present in the Vienna Genesis, though the stepped hills of the former convention and the town-symbols of the latter are not at first contiguous.[1] This suggests that the miniaturists combined information from pattern-books of two kinds: one, an Asianic compilation, providing specimens of rock-drawing and trees; the other, perhaps of Alexandrian or Antiochene origin, furnishing models for the towns. That pattern-books were extensively used in the Hellenistic period by painters and mosaicists, and therefore presumably also by book-illuminators, seems practically certain; it is highly probable that Petronius was alluding to them when he complained of the *compendiariae* of the Egyptians which were ruining the art of painting in his day.[2]

In Carolingian miniatures the confusion of the two methods is complete and perfectly unconscious, above all in the highly eclectic productions of the Saint-Denis school like the Bible of S. Callisto. The variety of landscape-treatment in this manuscript affords the best possible illustration of the hybrid nature of Carolingian art. For example, in the three Jerome scenes[3] alone we find bird's-eye views of towns and walled enclosures, horizon-seascapes cheek by jowl

[1] This only occurs, rather timidly, in the later miniatures: e.g. fols. 25–6.

[2] *Satyricon*, 2. 9: *pictura quoque non alium exitum fecit, postquam Aegyptiorum audacia tam magnae artis compendiariam inuenit.*

[3] Boinet, pl. 122.

with stepped hills in the *coulisse*-tradition, mushroom-topped trees like those in the Vienna Genesis, baldacchino-interiors, illusionist groves, and scalloped foregrounds: in other words, the whole repertory of antique landscape-motifs jumbled together into a completely irrational synthesis. It is clear that the artist has no interest whatever in the representation of space as such; he uses spatial metaphors merely as links to connect one narrative episode with another, and also, it may be, because these accessories had an ornamental value and gave an air of sophistication which he was unwilling to forgo. But in the presence of such compositions it is clearly beside the point to talk any longer of "picture space".

II

THE function of the frame in classical painting or relief sculpture is to define not only a surface-area but also a tract of space. It marks the limits of the imaginary scene in which the action takes place. It is not so much a window,[1] through which we view an infinite landscape, as the proscenium-opening, which regulates the height and breadth of the stage. For example, in the picture of the Death of Dido in the Vatican Virgil[2] the retreating lines of the coffered ceiling start from the top corners of the frame, and the picture surface is evidently imagined as a substitute for one wall of Dido's bedchamber. In a modern picture of an interior the artist is generally inside the room, like the figures he is painting; and the frame in consequence merely cuts off and isolates for aesthetic contemplation a tract of endless space. This idea of the frame as a window can only be realised completely when the representation of endless space has been systematised by the use of vanishing-point perspective.[3] As this was never scientifically worked out in ancient times, the only method of suggesting endless space was to extend the picture surface indefinitely to right and left. We thus reach the conception of the picture-roll as exemplified in the Vatican

[1] This conception of the frame appears in the writings of Renascence theorists like Alberti and Leonardo: see Panofsky, p. 291 f.

[2] Kömstedt, fig. 32.

[3] Panofsky, p. 270.

XVII. IVORY PANEL: THE ASCENSION
Darmstadt, Hessisches Landesmuseum.

Odyssey landscapes, the relief-band of the Column of Trajan, or the Joshua rotulus; and traces of originals designed on the same principle can be seen in the Utrecht Psalter and the Genesis scenes both in the Vienna MS. and in Carolingian bibles of the Tours school and their descendants. It will thus be observed that the continuous narrative style analysed by Wickhoff depends for its existence on this indefinite lateral extensibility of the pictorial field.[1]

At this point it becomes necessary to enquire whether we are justified in using the term picture space to describe the frieze-like area thus created. Greek dramatic convention, as is well known, demanded a unity of time and place;[2] and it is not difficult to show that Greek painting and relief-sculpture were equally strict. If the apparent exceptions, like the Telephus frieze from Pergamon,[3] are carefully examined, it will be seen that the alleged continuous landscape-setting is really nothing of the kind; the rocks and trees which separate the various episodes of the hero's life are not units in a co-ordinated landscape-scene, but picturesque substitutes for the ordinary geometrical borders of a relief-composition. Each separate episode enjoys an enclosed spatial and temporal unity; there is no spatial continuum throughout the whole frieze. In the Odyssey landscapes, on the other hand, the scene appears to be consistent although the events which it contains are consecutive in time; such a confusion is non-classical, and when we recollect that the character of the landscape is

[1] *Roman Art*, pp. 8 ff. [2] See Nicoll, *Development of the Theatre*, p. 37.
[3] *Altertümer von Pergamon*, iii. 2, pls. 31-2.

Alexandrian, we begin to suspect that the ancient oriental system of panoramic topography has returned to the Mediterranean world by way of Ptolemaic Egypt. Another monument of Alexandrian art, still more oriental in feeling, is the mosaic with Nilotic motifs in the Palazzo Barberini at Palestrina;[1] here again a number of episodes unconnected with each other are packed together in a continuous landscape-field without horizon and with only such attempt at recession as is implied by the diminution in the size of the figures towards the top of the composition. Perhaps a century and a half separate the Odyssey landscapes from the Palestrina mosaic;[2] within this period, the same as that which separates the paintings of the Boscoreale villa from the reliefs of the Column of Trajan, the effort to reconcile spatial and temporal extension is abandoned, and the time-factor is triumphant.

We have repeatedly insisted that Roman imperial art, like that of Assyria, Egypt, and India,[3] but unlike that of classical Greece, was a narrative art; and it was this habit of pictorial story-telling that it bequeathed to the medieval art of western Europe. Narrative, by its very nature, implies the predominance of the time-element; and every art which exists primarily for the sake of narrative must be ready to make sacrifices to this temporal factor. As the

[1] Schmidt, *Studien zum barberinischen Mosaik in Palestrina*; cf. Marucchi in *Bull. Com.* xxiii. (1895), pp. 32 ff.

[2] The theory that it belongs to the constructions of the Sullan period seems to be inadmissible on stylistic grounds: cf. Blake in *Mem. Amer. Acad. Rome*, viii. (1930), pp. 139 ff.

[3] Cf. Ippel, *Indische Kunst und Triumphalbild.*

adequate representation of space requires the absolute exclusion of time, owing to the fact that the vanishing-point perspective on which it depends requires a fixed and unvarying viewpoint, it is inevitable that narrative art must sacrifice its curiosity about space. Thus the frame, except at the top and bottom, plays no essential part in narrative representation; its function of defining and limiting a closed tract of space is unwelcome to an art which has no concern with space as such and resents lateral limitation. It will thus appear that the frame in narrative art becomes a mere mechanical convenience, and exercises no control over the contents of the area it surrounds.[1]

Since the exigencies of the frame as a controller of spatial relationships are now removed, it follows that the whole problem of design is now concentrated upon the organisation of the picture surface. The painted page and the carved panel now become the primary data, not the imaginary space which they had metaphorically to reproduce; and the artist is now absorbed with the rhythm of lines and the play of colours for their own sake. In the last chapter it became increasingly evident that the effort to master an ideal space was too great a burden for the Carolingian artist; if the problem had been satisfactorily solved by his teachers, it is possible that the medieval painter might have utilised the solution successfully, just as certain Japanese printmakers adopted European perspective to good effect,[2] but as the antique painters themselves were far from competent to deal

[1] Cf. Panofsky, p. 272.

[2] E.g. Kiyotada, in his *Interior of a Tea-House*.

adequately with the third dimension and themselves lost interest in the subject, their Carolingian successors can hardly be blamed for their failure to advance the technical study of spatial representation.

As designers in two dimensions Carolingian book-painters and ivory-carvers display the characteristic northern talent for producing baroque effects of texture and calligraphic fantasies. We shall examine a representative series of miniatures and ivories from this point of view and observe how the further ninth-century artists departed from their late-antique models and the more familiar they grew with the merely mechanical aspects of representational art, the more original and surprising their transformations of late-antique motifs appear. From antiquity Carolingian artists learned how to construct the figure as a plastic unit and how to arrange such units in a plausible context. They discovered a certain rather limited number of formulas and poses, certain schemes of proportion, certain methods of organising space which enabled them to satisfy their need for a ready-made didactic and narrative art. But if we compare the Carolingian copy with the late-antique model we perceive at once that the medieval artist has borrowed from his ancient predecessor only the skeleton of his art, and that the flesh and garments with which he clothed that framework are of his own invention. The actual methods of drawing a line or cutting a surface are his own. There is hardly ever any doubt as to whether a given ivory is a late-antique piece of the fifth or sixth century or a Carolingian copy of the ninth. The iconographic elements may

XVIII. APOCALYPTIC SCENE: MINIATURE FROM THE CODEX AUREUS FROM ST. EMMERAM AT REGENSBURG
Munich, Bayerische Staatsbibliothek.

be the same, and the general notion of the scene may even be borrowed directly; but the idiom and accent change. It is like the difference between a native's and a foreigner's way of speaking the same language. The student and critic of Carolingian style has to learn how to detect and analyse these subtle variations of tone, pitch, and tempo, since it is there, and not in what he has to say, that the medieval artist reveals both his own individuality and the mental tenour of his age. The stock of ideas and the phraseology in which they are expressed are borrowed from antiquity, but the accent is that of the ninth century and of northern Europe.

The three most notable aesthetic features of Carolingian art are its use of pattern and texture, its love of linear effects, and its sense of material. All these denote an art of surfaces, and in all the northern tradition is conspicuous. The Hellenistic art of the Mediterranean world, being interested in imitation and little else besides, neglected pattern because it was primarily concerned with the correct presentation of the individual elements in a spatial connexion; it neglected linear effects because it saw figures and other bodies as plastic units, and was only secondarily occupied with contours; and it neglected the peculiar qualities of a given material because the substance out of which a work of art was made had no function except to make an abstract idea accessible to the senses. It will be seen, therefore, that if Carolingian artists had come into direct contact with pre-Christian Greek art, they would have found it as unmanageable and unconvincing as their Celtic and Germanic precursors had done. Mediterranean art was only valuable to the Nordic artist of the ninth century because it had already been dematerialised by an oriental religion and barbaric tastes from the second to the sixth centuries, while still retaining the humanist inclination and the imitative facility which the anthropophobic art of the North required for the service of Christianity.

The first characteristic of Carolingian art just mentioned, its use of pattern and texture, reminds us in some respects of the baroque phase of Roman relief-sculpture studied in the second chapter. Once more we find the congestion, the absence of background, the suggestion of spiritual excitement by means of an airless super-objectivity which we noted in the Ludovisi battle-sarcophagus in the Museo Nazionale in Rome. In the remarkable ivory at Darmstadt[1] representing the Virgin and the Apostles witnessing the Ascension the figures are packed together in a dense crowd which, in the absence of the formal border, seems like a tiny detachment broken away from an infinitely large struggling mass of humanity. This tremendous tension has nothing to do with physical confinement in a narrow space; it seems to come from within, drawing the bodies together as though by magnetic force and lifting them off their feet by its intensity. The original of this composition was probably an Alexandrian or Byzantine carving of the sixth century, in the style of the New Testament scenes on the back of the throne of Maximian at Ravenna, but the bland manner of the

Plate XVII opp. p. 178

[1] Goldschmidt, i. 20.

late-antique work has been strangely transformed into this ecstatic design. The emotional power is not suggested by facial expression; the physiognomic types are rather conventional and consciously archaising. It seems to be conveyed partly by the rhythm of the tightly packed bodies, with their heads and haloes screwed round to watch the miracle, and partly by the turbulence of the draperies. This use of inanimate accessories to heighten the dramatic effect is even more noticeable in the Leipzig ivory of the Archangel Michael[1] slaying the dragon; the twirl of drapery round the shaft of his spear, the rope-like folds of his garment, and even small details like the fluted nimbus, the scaly cuffs, and the beaded bands of ornament are extraordinarily effective in giving a dynamic quality to the whole design. The action of the figure does, of course, justify the dramatic treatment, but it does not condition it. As a matter of fact the attitude of the Leipzig Archangel to the dragon is extremely perfunctory; his spear rests lightly in the dragon's mouth and is gracefully held in position, but not grasped or thrust, by his long and elegant right hand, while his feet, which are supposed to be trampling on the reptile, in fact dangle idly above its head. Thus if we analyse the action, it is in itself quite unconvincing; the life of the figure is purely abstract and ornamental.

Plate V opp. p. 42

This command of rhythmic movement enables the Carolingian artist on occasion to achieve effects quite beyond the range of men trained in the classical schools. The Munich Codex Aureus from St.

[1] Goldschmidt, i. 11.

Plate XVIII opp. p. 182 Emmeram at Regensburg contains a miniature of the twenty-four Elders of the Apocalypse adoring the Lamb.[1] They are grouped before him in a great hemicycle; their attitudes of ecstasy are identical, and this concerted act of worship has the moving power of a vast choir in an oratorio. As we noted apropos of the processions of saints in Sant' Apollinare Nuovo at Ravenna, the artists of Byzantium and the east understood perfectly the spiritual implications of a single gesture repeated exactly over and over again; the Frankish artist improved on this ritual by charging it with all the dramatic and emotional intensity of his race. Again it will be seen that this spiritual excitement is awakened by almost abstract means. The theoretical space of sky in which the Lamb appears has hardly even an imaginary existence; the Elders too, crammed together in a sort of garland of humanity, exist entirely on the surface of the page. Once more the effect is produced by pattern and texture, not by imitative means.

The emancipation of Carolingian art from the antique conventions of space is completed in the second half of the ninth century. The Apocalyptic scene in the Munich Codex Aureus (*c.* 870) is typical of all the more important miniatures and ivories of this period in its disregard of depth and its determination to project all the action on to the single plane of the picture surface. If we examine, for instance, the scenes from the life of Moses in the Bible of San Callisto[2] we find a total lack of spatial continuity. Not only are episodes separated in time crowded

[1] Boinet, pl. 116. [2] Boinet, pls. 123-4.

together in the same frame, but also the accessories jostle and intrude upon each other in a disconcerting fashion. The only divisions between the episodes are snatches of shaded ground which sometimes does for clouds and sometimes for rocks, but which is as unimportant objectively as the meaningless fluted conches inserted behind the heads of the archbishop and the deacons in the Cambridge liturgical ivory. It is interesting to see that the practice of indicating the direction of a plane by a sharp and arbitrary gradation of tone is here used precisely as it is by El Greco, Cézanne, and the early cubists. The device is borrowed, of course, from the chiaroscuro of the rocks in a *coulisse*-landscape, but it is employed for expressionist, not for representational purposes.

The arrangement of figures in irregular tiers which we find in the miniatures of the Saint-Denis school, and especially in the Bible of San Callisto, as well as in the ivories of the Liuthard and later Metz groups, is commonly spoken of as a kind of bird's-eye view. This is not quite correct. The bird's-eye view, as used in Odyssey landscapes in the Vatican, implies a consistent attitude to space and has a kind of subjective logic. In these Carolingian compositions, however, there is no such consistency, the primary fact is the painted or carved surface and on to this are projected as many figures as the surface will conveniently carry. These figures have no spatial attributes, such as weight; they need no ground to tread on, beyond a conventional little frill immediately under their feet, and they are supported partly by leaning upon one another and partly because they are one with the background to which they are attached. Unlike the figures in an antique relief of the classical period, they are not imagined as separate from the panel which physically sustains them; like the architectural sculpture on a Romanesque cathedral they are still part of the body from which they emerge. This attitude to form is best illustrated by a concrete example; a section of the Passion diptych in the Cathedral Treasury at Milan[1] is here reproduced in its natural size, in order to show the relation of figure to ground. It will be observed that all the heads are in the same plane, even though their bodies may overlap. This means that the background is at different depths in different places: deeply excavated within the building to the left and behind the mushroom-headed trees, quite near the surface in the rocks on which the Apostles stand while Christ appears to them. This irregularity is, of course, found in Greek reliefs of the fifth century B.C.—the Parthenon frieze, for instance; but whereas it is there concealed, the ground being merely necessary to support the figures and having no positive character of its own, here its uneven surface is insisted upon and converted into a positive virtue. The figures, the ground, and the accessories like the trees and buildings appear as different aspects of the same primary substance, the ivory panel on which the scene is carved. This organic continuity of material is

Plate XIX

[1] Goldschmidt regards this diptych as a work of the fifth century: text p. 13 and fig. 9. But the arrangement of the figures, as well as details of dress, architecture, etc., make this impossible. See Weigand in *Kritische Berichte*, 1930–31, p. 49. The figure-compositions are imitated on the Ottonian situla now in the Victoria and Albert Museum (Goldschmidt, ii. 3).

XIX. DETAIL FROM IVORY DIPTYCH WITH SCENES FROM THE PASSION
Milan, Cathedral Treasury.

the medieval substitute for the ideal continuity of space in the antique relief.

The same surface-continuity really prevails also in works which at first sight seem to be designed in spatial terms like the Cambridge and Frankfort liturgical panels. The meaningless changes of scale from the little castellated walls at the top and bottom of the Cambridge leaf[1] to the singing deacons, and again from them to the priest, betray an art which is essentially non-naturalistic, for all its careful life-like detail. It can only be compared with the design of those sixth-century Byzantine diptychs which we have noted as among the first fully developed examples of the conceptual, transcendental art of the Middle Ages.

The oriental art of pure surface, to which these late Carolingian objects approximate in intention, may be seen still more completely in the golden altar of Sant' Ambrogio in Milan,[2] that one supreme masterpiece which survives to show what the ninth century could achieve when it turned from the making of delightful things to hold in the hand and created a work on a monumental scale. In this we observe those other two characteristics of Carolingian art mentioned just now—its love of linear effects and its instinct for material splendour—developed to their highest pitch.

Plate XX opp. p. 192

The front of the altar, facing the congregation, is entirely of gold, except for the narrow band of fret-

[1] Goldschmidt, i. 120.

[2] Tarchiani in *Dedalo*, ii. (1921), pp. 5 ff. Venturi, *Storia dell' arte italiana*, ii. pp. 233 ff.

pattern along the top and the acanthus-border along the bottom, which are of silver. The three main panels are separated by narrow strips of enamel; and within these panels the small compartments are likewise edged with enamel and studded at intervals with rubies, amethysts, moonstones, and other gems, as well as with a number of antique cameos. The front facing the choir and the celebrant is chiefly of silver, though broad gold mouldings frame the three main panels, and thin gold beadings and filigree mounts for the jewels give a suffused glow to the pale moonlight colour of the ground. The figure-subjects, moreover, are heightened with gold; and again enamel-bands and jewels add to the splendour of the effect. A fresh note is struck here by the niello inscription on the silver band that surrounds the three main panels. The two ends of the altar are treated in the same way as the front facing the choir, partly in silver and partly in gold; but the enamel is here especially conspicuous, as it fills the arms of the large crosses in the centre of each end.

The balance of line, colour, and texture is managed with consummate taste. The subdivision of the sides is ingeniously varied; and in all cases the proportions of the figure-subjects and ornament to the panels, and of the panels to the whole side, are admirably contrived. Gold and silver are perfectly contrasted; and the jewels, beautiful in themselves, are never forced upon our attention, but seem to flower effortlessly in the appropriate context. The enamel, moreover, is extremely successful, though very simple: opaque white and turquoise blue, transparent emerald green, and rare touches of garnet red. The blue is more noticeable in the angle-pilasters.

This complex harmony of colour immediately stands out as something non-Mediterranean. No antique artist was capable of such bold and yet delicate chromatic invention. There is a wide gulf between the single melodic line of classical art and this elaborate orchestration of silver and gold, enamel and jewels. The only comparable works are Byzantine objects like the so-called Ewer of Charlemagne at Saint Maurice d'Agaune [1] in Switzerland or the Beresford Hope Cross in the Victoria and Albert Museum,[2] or Celtic and Saxon manuscripts like the Book of Kells and the Lindisfarne Gospels.

We have already noted the theory that the Magister Wolvinius who signed this magnificent work was none other than the "Vussin" who appears as a pupil of Einhard in one of his letters; it would be pleasant to see the genius of the Beseleel of Aachen thus glowing in the background. But this must remain a guess. What is more certain is that the donor of the altar, one Angilbertus, was the bishop of that name who occupied the See of Milan from 824 to 829; and there are reasons for thinking that he made his most splendid gift to the basilica of St. Ambrose about 835. There is too little comparative material to enable us to confirm this dating on internal grounds. The gold repoussé cover [3] of the Munich Codex Aureus is similar in style to the miniatures, and was produced like them at Saint-Denis about 870. The resemblance between

[1] Rosenberg, *Zellenschmelz*, iii. pp. 22 ff. [2] *Ibid.*, iii. pp. 53 ff.
[3] Hauttmann, *Kunst des frühen Mittelalters*, p. 338.

this and the Milan altar is not at all close. In some respects the relation of the figure-subjects to their setting is nearer to that of the antependium in the cathedral at Aachen, a work of the last quarter of the tenth century; and it is sometimes suggested that the Milan altar, like the ciborium over it, is actually a work of the Ottonian period. The comparisons with the Metz Sacramentary and the Bible of San Callisto made by other authorities involve an inconvenient time-lag of about fifty years, if the dating *c.* 835 is correct. On the other hand, certain features point to the influence of Byzantine art, especially the jewelled footstools, the beds, the architectural accessories, and other minor details; though the figure-style is distinctively Frankish. Perhaps we must assume that Wolvinius was trained in the north—at Aachen, or possibly at Rheims—and when in Milan came into contact with some of the east Christian models which exercised so important an influence on Ottonian art. Only thus, it seems, can we explain the curious mixture of Frankish and Byzantine elements.

The formal principle of the figure panels is essentially linear; the modelled surfaces are defined by sharp ridges which catch the light, and the contours are frequently emphasised by fine dotted lines. The representational elements—whether human beings, trees or buildings—are isolated like islands in the sea of gold. They do not stand on the ground and detach themselves against empty space; they float, as it were, half submerged in a glowing viscous fluid. This is exactly the same in effect as the gold background of Byzantine mosaics, enamels, and miniatures: that ideal

XX. DETAIL FROM THE GOLDEN ALTAR OF ANGILBERT
Milan, Sant' Ambrogio.

envelope which, as we saw in the second chapter, was deliberately intended to destroy the illusion of the sensible world. This oriental *mise-en-scène* is comparatively uncommon in Carolingian painting; it seems rather to make its way into western art through metalwork and ivory-carving. It appears in a modified form in the Majestas of Tours Bibles; and even regulates to some extent the layout of the David picture and the dedication scene in the Vivian Bible, which make no attempt to provide a spatial setting for their figure-action. But the gold ground is not used in Carolingian art unless it is the actual material of the surface which carries the representation.

The extreme linear precision of the figures on the Milan altar is partly conditioned by the material and form of the object in question, but it is also a general characteristic of Carolingian, as of all Nordic, representational art. The illusionist style of late-antique painting and the solidly modelled style of late-antique relief are reduced to a series of calligraphic formulas which will lie easily on the all-important surface. The figure-drawings in the Utrecht Psalter demonstrate convincingly how this flattening and disembodying process can be achieved without sacrificing the plausibility of the representation. On the contrary, its vitality and dynamic rhythm are actually enhanced by translating the pictorial convention into pure draughtsmanship. The imitative rendering of colour and texture in the late-antique model is replaced by an expressionist technique of brisk penstrokes. The ancient artist had aimed at representing self-contained repose and suggesting a static atmosphere, whereas the medieval artist liked violent movement, vivacious gestures, and a general air of bustle and excitement. This has little to do with the inherent character of the scene he was depicting; it seems to be inseparable from his whole manner of envisaging form. Even where there is no human interest, the northern style is essentially dramatic. The animal interlacing on the Oseberg ship, for example, has an immediately exciting quality, like the sound of a horn. This inner activity finds, of course, a fuller scope when it is allowed to exercise itself upon a human subject; and Carolingian art swarms with figures whose animation seems almost diabolic. A recent writer[1] has remarked that the figures in the Utrecht Psalter look as if they were dancing a perpetual tarantella, with their craning necks, goggling eyes, and draperies all a-flutter in the wind that wrenches the trees about and sweeps the very landscape into a cloud of dust.

This episodic and non-organic method of composition appears in its most extreme form on the engraved crystal disk in the British Museum which bears the name of the emperor Lothair;[2] there is little pretence here even at surface-coherence, and the little groups seem to have come together quite at random in the circular area. On closer inspection, however, they are seen to be instinctively well proportioned and well placed, and to form a kind of open mesh as effective in its way as the densely textured miniatures and ivories are in theirs. A similar, but not so felicitous

Plate XI opp. p. 122

[1] Tarchiani, *op. cit.*, p. 24.
[2] Dalton, *Cat. of Engraved Gems*, no. 559, pl. xix.

use of scattered units within a circle occurs in the Autun Sacramentary,[1] a Tours MS. which borrows its decorative motifs from metalwork and the minor arts, not from late-antique book-painting.

The northern principle of composing by surface-texture rather than by the co-ordination of masses or the rhythmic organisation of lines is thus applied to the rationalist figure art of the Mediterranean. It had been developed to a remarkable pitch of perfection in purely ornamental work like the decorated pages of Celtic and Anglo-Saxon manuscripts as well as in Germanic metalwork, but its suitability to representational art had never been systematically investigated. Hints of it are seen in late Antonine reliefs like that on the Ludovisi battle-sarcophagus and on those exceptional ivories like the pierced Bellerophon panel in the British Museum[2] or the diptych with Dionysiac subjects at Sens;[3] but these must be regarded as anomalous in the antique world, where the physical solidity and opacity of the object decorated was almost an article of faith. So consistent is this law even in Carolingian objects derived from the antique that we can estimate the Nordic element most easily in just those pieces which deny the antique principle of opacity in the most outspoken way.

One of the earliest of these pieces is the pair of ivory bookcovers from Genoels-Elderen in Brussels.[4] On account of the resemblance between the facial types on these panels and those on the chalice of

[1] Boinet, pl. 43. [2] Dalton, *Cat. of Ivories*, no. 6, pl. iii.
[3] Peirce and Tyler, *L'art byzantin*, i. pl. 121.
[4] Goldschmidt, i. 1-2.

Tassilo at Kremsmünster,[1] which is datable between 777 and 788, the Brussels covers belong to the last quarter of the eighth century. The figures are flat and linear in manner and show no influence of the antique plastic style revived by the artists of the Ada school; they are cut out round their contours and attached to the frame only by means of the architectural and other accessories, and on the back cover even the frame is made of two thin strips joined at intervals by knots of strapwork. The ivory is treated as if it were a sheet of metal; and it is probable that this curious technique was actually suggested by goldsmiths' work, presumably in that filigree style which had long been popular in the north. Precisely the same formal instinct is apparent in the two pierced covers of an Evangelistary from Metz in the Bibliothèque Nationale,[2] one of which is reproduced here.[3] The individual elements are now more plastically treated, of course; but the manner of linking figures to architecture and architecture to frame is exactly like that of the Brussels covers, which are nearly a hundred years earlier. The presence of the Asiatic mushroom-headed tree both on this and on the Bellerophon panel, in addition to the pierced technique, might suggest that the Paris ivories were derived from just such a Syrian prototype of the fifth century; but the iconography of the Massacre of

Plate XXI

[1] Riegl, *Spätrömische Kunstindustrie*, ii. pp. 53 ff., pls. xxii.-xxv.; Baldwin Brown, *Arts in Early England*, vi. pp. 79 ff.

[2] Goldschmidt, i. 72-3.

[3] Fonds latin, 9388; Goldschmidt no. 72 is at present attached to another Metz MS., the Gospel-book lat. 9393, but the two covers originally belonged to the same book.

XXI. IVORY BOOKCOVER: ANNUNCIATION; ADORATION OF THE MAGI; MASSACRE OF THE INNOCENTS
Paris, Bibliothèque Nationale.

the Innocents is western, being especially associated with those ivories which Baldwin Smith ascribes to Provence.[1] This eclecticism is characteristic of Metz ivories.

The pierced technique of the Paris bookcovers is combined with the classical convention of relief on a later masterpiece of the Metz school, the liturgical comb of St. Heribert now in the Schnütgen Museum at Cologne.[2] The Crucifixion occupies a plain ground; but to right and left are two rose-windows, and above are two angels, partly seen against the solid ground and partly involved with the great acanthus-scrolls in the openwork style which form the upper part of the design. This mixture of decorative void and decorated solid shows clearly that the Carolingian artist thought only in terms of surface and silhouette, and revealed his essentially Nordic attitude to form precisely in this refusal to distinguish ground from pattern.

Plate XXII opp. p. 198

[1] The executioners smash the children down, instead of piercing them with a sword: cf. *Early Christian Iconography*, pp. 62 ff.

[2] Goldschmidt, i. 92a.

III

THE natural result of this reduction of the plastic or pictorial scene to a piece of surface-decoration was that the classical distinction between image and ornament tended to disappear from medieval book-illumination. So long as there was a psychological difference between what was seen *through* the page (in the miniatures) and what was seen *on* the page (the text, with its ornaments), the two aspects of the book remained separate and parallel. This antique division survived in Byzantine art, where image and ornament obeyed each their own laws and made few mutual concessions. In the west, however, ornament began at an early date to play a more important part than it ever played in the Byzantine world; and when the Carolingian artists introduced a narrative style of book-painting from Mediterranean lands, they had to accommodate their figure-subjects to the ornamental system which refused to be displaced. It is the aim of this final chapter to show how the rival claims of illustration and decoration were reconciled in Carolingian art.

In a Celtic manuscript like the Book of Kells illustration hardly exists; the few figure-subjects are so completely ornamentalised that their didactic value is of the slightest. In a book like the Vienna Genesis, on the other hand, the primary function of the pictures is to provide a commentary to the text, and their decorative value is a minor consideration. It was

XXII. IVORY COMB OF ST. HERIBERT
Cologne, Schnütgenmuseum.

the object of Carolingian book-painting to combine the advantages of both these systems into a single unity. At first this was done by mixing up Mediterranean illusionistic figure-compositions with Celtic and Germanic ornament, each technique retaining its character more or less unaltered. For example, in a Tours MS. like the Vivian Bible the miniatures are, as we have seen, partly based on prototypes of the fifth century and partly, it would seem, original creations of the ninth, whereas the ornament of the canon-tables is a mixture of classical acanthus, palmette, and vine with northern interlacing strapwork and oriental "sacred-tree" finials and fanciful motifs taken from coins and gems and metalwork.[1] This jumble of incompatible elements produces an effect which is frankly barbarous; and from the aesthetic point of view the manuscript as a whole cannot be called a success, however interesting it may be in detail.

The extreme eclecticism of Tours manuscripts was avoided by the artists of the Ada school, who concentrated on a more architectural scheme and maintained a more consistent scale of treatment in all parts of the book. Having set the pace by adopting the elaborately coloured and modelled Evangelist-portrait, they converted the arcading of the canon-tables, which had become progressively more and more attenuated and schematic,[2] into realistic structures

[1] The ornament of Tours MSS. is exhaustively studied by Köhler in the first volume of his book, *Die karolingischen Miniaturen: Die Schule von Tours.*

[2] The antique plastic type of arcading survived in Italy as late as the eighth century: see the British Museum Gospels from San Vincenzo al Volturno (Add. MSS. 5463) datable to 739–60.

with rounded columns of porphyry and other variegated stones, Corinthian capitals, and arches adorned with the traditional mouldings. The page here *Plate XXIII* illustrated, from the Harley Gospels in the British Museum,[1] shows an arcade with alternating straight and helical columns, the latter being adorned with little human figures—apparently cupids vintaging—and deriving from an actual carved prototype like the famous *columna vitinea* in Rome, traditionally supposed to have been that against which Christ was scourged.[2] The capitals, moreover, though somewhat fantasticated, are not essentially different from actual carved capitals found at Lorsch and elsewhere.[3] The brilliant polychrome effects—green, blue, violet, orange, and other colours arranged in spots, veins, and stripes—are doubtless a painted reflection of the marble intarsia and mosaic which, as we know from literary sources, once adorned the interiors of the great Carolingian basilicas. This liking for patterned architecture, it may be noted in passing, was not indulged on the inside only; the gate-house at Lorsch,[4] for instance, is covered with a diaper of hexagonal and triangular tiles which produces an almost oriental effect.

Even the initials and ornamental text-pages in Ada MSS. maintain successfully this architectonic scale. In the early members of the group, such as the Gospels from Saint-Denis in the Bibliothèque

[1] Boinet, pl. 12.

[2] Chapot, *La colonne torse*, p. 144.

[3] Meyer-Barkhausen in *Zeitschr. f. bild. Kunst*, lxiii. (1929), pp. 126 ff.

[4] Behn in *Forschungen und Fortschritte*, 20 Oct. 1933, pp. 433 ff.

XXIII. CANON-TABLE FROM THE HARLEY GOSPELS
London, British Museum.

Nationale (lat. 9387),[1] the Psalter of Charles the Great in Vienna (cod. 1861),[2] the Abbeville Gospels (cod. 1),[3] or the Gospels from Saint-Martin-des-Champs in the Bibliothèque de l'Arsenal (cod. 599),[4] the text-ornament of the *incipit*-pages follows the general plan of the same feature in insular manuscripts. The asymmetric effect, however, which is so conspicuous in the Book of Kells or the Lindisfarne Gospels, is here mitigated by setting the initial and the decorative text on a rectangular purple ground and enclosing this in a regular geometric frame like that which surrounds the Evangelist-portraits. In the developed MSS. of the Ada group this architectonic tendency is confirmed; and the initial letters are treated as if they were solid objects placed within a niche. For instance the Q of the word *Quoniam* which begins the Gospel according to St. Luke is fitted symmetrically under the arch in the Harley-codex;[5] in the Gospels of Saint-Médard[6] it is placed to the side, but is still organised as though it were part of the architecture. In both the last instances the loop of the Q becomes an oval frame containing a separate and complete miniature.

Plate XXIV opp. p. 206

This use of the initial-letter as the frame or support for a figure-subject, which became so popular a feature of western medieval book-painting, is first developed extensively in the Drogo Sacramentary.[7] The letter is no longer an abstract symbol, a mere geometric figure. It becomes a trellis round which scrolls of acanthus are twined, or a wall with towers,

[1] Boinet, pl. 5. [2] Boinet, pl. 6. [3] Boinet, pl. 9.
[4] Boinet, pl. 11. [5] Boinet, pl. 14. [6] Boinet, pl. 23.
[7] Boinet, pls. 86-90; completely illustrated in Weber, *op. cit.*, pls. 1-28.

or some such objective metaphor; and the human figures are either perched on the upright members of the initials, or accommodated inside them, or else they are grouped in the usual way into a miniature composition within the enclosed area of a D or some such letter. The ambiguity of the relationship of figure-scene to frame still survives in this last case. The conception of the letter as a trellis or scaffold is logically intelligible, but it is less easy to decide whether the closed letters are to be thought of as frames through which we look at a scene beyond, or whether they are simply boundaries which define a certain surface-area. In the Drogo Sacramentary the figures and landscape-accessories are drawn and coloured in a wash-technique half-way between the solidly modelled body-colour of the Ada MSS. and the tinted drawings of the St. Gall Golden Psalter; this technical compromise perhaps implies a mental compromise between the pictorial and linear, or Mediterranean and Nordic, conceptions of form. At any rate, it is convenient so to regard it.

The purely northern tradition of abstract ornament plays an important, though restricted, part in the decoration of Carolingian books. It occurs incidentally in the initial-letters of manuscripts whose figure-subjects are derived from late-antique sources, such as the Gospel-books of the Ada school and the bibles and psalters of Tours. In only one group of manuscripts, however—those of the so-called Franco-Saxon school—is the abstract linear style responsible for the main decorative effect. These manuscripts probably originated in a monastery of north-western

France, perhaps that of Saint-Vaast at Arras.[1] They appear about the middle of the ninth century; among the earlier productions of this school are the second bible of Charles the Bald[2] and the Gospels of Francis II,[3] both in the Bibliothèque Nationale. The decoration of these books consists chiefly of elaborate initials and geometric frames and surface-divisions of various kinds. Their structural principles have recently been analysed by Nordenfalk,[4] who observes that the trend of design is from the static to the dynamic and from the closed to the open. In other words, the classical principle gives way to the baroque. The early manuscripts of the Franco-Saxon school show purist tendencies in the design of their initials; their structure is self-contained and organically clear, and their ornament is well under control. It may be fantastic in conception, as in a Gospel-book in the Bibliothèque Nationale (lat. 11956),[5] with its strange monsters at the foot of the canon-tables, whose arcades rest on columns interrupted in the middle by rings and acanthus-loops and topped by capitals stylised out of recognition; but the actual handling is solid and decided, as though the material were positive enough. By the time we reach the Echternach Sacramentary,[6] however, which dates from the end of the ninth century, the initials have become a maze of lines without architectonic coherence, a sort of

[1] Cf. the Evangelistary from that house, now in the municipal library at Arras (cod. 1045): Boinet, pls. 93-6.

[2] Boinet, pls. 100-102.

[3] Boinet, pls. 97-9.

[4] In *Acta Archaeologica*, ii. (1931), pp. 207 ff.

[5] Nordenfalk, *op. cit.*, p. 243, fig. 20.

[6] Bibliothèque Nationale, lat. 9433: Nordenfalk, *op. cit.*, pp. 208 ff.

cat's cradle lacking all rigidity and substance. The panels of plaitwork, moreover, which once were securely jointed into the trunk of the letter, now seem to float in a fluid, like the little index in a maximum-and-minimum thermometer, to which Nordenfalk happily compares them.

This disintegration of the letter into pure ornament is but one aspect of that process which is periodically repeated in the art of northern Europe. A wider application of the same principle is seen in the medieval artist's attitude to the frame which he inherited from antique art. In antiquity the frame is either a strip with a longitudinal pattern such as the cable or bead-and-reel, or a moulding whose elements—such as the acanthus-leaf or egg-and-dart—face uniformly inwards towards the area enclosed. The former alternative is historically the earlier, though it survives alongside what we may call the centripetal frame, which seems to have been introduced into Greek art about the middle of the fourth century B.C.[1] Both agree in regarding each side of the frame as a single and indivisible unit, even if only a section of an infinite strip or moulding. In northern art, however, this organic continuity of the frame is disregarded, especially in book-painting; and it becomes a mere border patched together out of odd fragments with no inner cohesion among themselves. The artist of the Lindisfarne Gospels, for instance, accepts the principle of the ruled border if it suits his purpose, but makes as little of it as need be; the most complicated

[1] See the moulded panels on the dodecagonal column-base from the Didymaion at Miletus: Pontremoli and Haussoullier, *Didymes*, pl. xv.

interlacings, which might go on for ever, come suddenly to an end in a non-committal boundary line.

Since the frame ceases to have any positive character it is not surprising to find what are really parts of the content turning into a sort of improvised margin. An instance of this confusion may be seen on the ivory panel of St. Gregory at Heiligenkreuz:[1] the figure is set between the traditional columns and looped curtains; but above, instead of the proper arch, we have a city wall with towers and a gate. The bold combination of the setting, which is part of the picture, with the frame, which surrounds it, is typically medieval; and we can see in the architectural headpiece the ancestor of the town-canopies above the heads of Romanesque statues. This attitude to the frame is so significant that it could be made into a test of the artist's education and sympathies.

The frames of Carolingian ivory-carvings follow the traditional antique patterns more faithfully than the frames of the miniatures, which introduce northern elements quite freely. The favourite border is the row of overlapping acanthus-leaves; this is relatively uncommon in antiquity, being practically confined to western ivories of the fifth century. In the ninth century it becomes very elaborate, especially in the later period; in Liuthard ivories the leaves are thin and delicate and very much undercut, while the Metz carvers prefer a richer, denser, and more massive form of leaf. Although the motif is antique, it is now put to fresh uses; the ornamental effect of the frame is cultivated for its own sake, as we see in

[1] Goldschmidt, i. 122.

the beautiful openwork vine-border of the Metz bookcover in the Bibliothèque Nationale. This vogue for the vine as a decorative motif, which had begun in late antiquity, is very marked in Anglo-Saxon England;[1] and its popularity in Carolingian art was probably not exclusively due to the influence of late antique ivories, for it is not common on the western ivories most in favour with Frankish carvers, and it is uncertain whether Syro-Egyptian models like the decorative panels of the throne of Maximian were accessible in the north during the ninth century. It is possible that textiles may have helped to diffuse the motif;[2] but it is less usual on the Byzantine and Sasanian silks which were so eagerly collected in the north than on the earlier and more commonplace woollen textiles of Coptic Egypt which were not so often exported.

This characteristically northern passion for ornament was not easily confined to borders, however prominent and elaborate; and we find complete pages of illuminated manuscripts and whole ivory panels given up to acanthus-scrolls and other such patterns. The principle of the decorative page was well established in Germanic and Celtic art; the novelty consisted in substituting for the abstract spirals and interlacings of northern art the organic scrolls and tendrils and garlands of the south. We have already seen how in the *Incipit*-pages of Ada MSS. the decorative text is converted into a kind of

[1] The development is studied in detail by Bröndsted, *Early English Ornament*, pp. 16 ff.

[2] Cf. the Cluny panels: Goldschmidt, i. 156–7.

XXIV. ORNAMENTAL PAGE FROM THE GOSPELS OF SAINT-MARTIN-DES-CHAMPS
Paris, Bibliothèque de l'Arsenal.

independent image of equal value to the Evangelist-portraits; this principle is carried a step further in the two great Saint-Denis MSS., the Munich Codex Aureus,[1] and the Bible of San Callisto,[2] where the writing is simply smothered in a jungle of leafage and interlacing.

As before, the ivory-carvers are more restrained than the book-painters; and the purely decorative panels observe a certain moderation which is not found in the ornamental manuscript-pages. All the same, the ornamental element becomes increasingly prominent in later Carolingian ivories, particularly those made in the Alemannic regions, at St. Gall and Reichenau, and perhaps also at Milan. The best known among these later pieces are the Tuotilo book-covers at St. Gall[3], which, if not necessarily made by the monk of that name who flourished between 895 and 912, certainly belong to just that period. Above the figure-subjects on both these panels are broad bands filled with symmetrically linked acanthus-scrolls, which somewhat resemble those on a silver-gilt covered cup of about the same date in the British Museum.[4] The figure-subjects—a Majestas with the symbols of the Evangelists, Earth and Ocean, and Cherubim on one cover, the Assumption of the Virgin and an episode from the Life of St. Gall on the other—are neither more nor less important from the aesthetic point of view than the scrolls of acanthus. Image and ornament are at last completely equated.

[1] Boinet, pls. 119-20. [2] Boinet, pls. 129-30. [3] Goldschmidt, i. 163.
[4] Read and Tonnochy, *Cat. of Silver Plate in the Franks Bequest*, no. 98.

It would be difficult to find any work of ancient art of which this could be said. There are plenty of examples of Hellenistic and Roman decorative art where the human beings are subordinate to the ornament; but in these cases the human beings are always conventional types—victories or cupids, not historical personages. One of the few exceptions to this rule, which applies at least till the fifth century, is the Antioch chalice; and even here the very fact that the figures among the vine-scrolls represent Christ and the Apostles has been used as an argument against its authenticity.[1] This mixture of the human and the vegetable in the same field does not, of course, apply to the Tuotilo ivories, where the figure-subjects and acanthus-scrolls are confined to separate zones; what strikes us as significant, however, is that in the Tuotilo panels there is no change of scale, ethical or aesthetic, when we pass from the ornament to the image and back again to the ornament. Not only is there no suggestion that one genre is subordinate to the other, but there is actually a formal sympathy between them. The ribs on the acanthus-leaves produce the same effect of texture as the fine pleated folds of the draperies; and on either panel the curves of the acanthus-scrolls allude to the curved span of the angels' and cherubim's wings. This extremely felicitous adjustment of tone, texture, and rhythm is only possible in an art which accepts the decorative

[1] Morey in *Art Studies* (1925), pp. 73 ff. The argument, except as far as the objection to an early (first century) dating is concerned, loses its weight after the fifth century, since there is in the Istanbul museum (Mendel, *Cat.* no. 659) a carved drum with the baptism of Christ thus placed among vine-scrolls.

surface as its primary datum and which refuses to differentiate between the aesthetic values of image and ornament.

It will be seen, therefore, that by the end of the ninth century the decisive principles of western European medieval art had already been formulated. From the material point of view the Carolingians concentrated on what are called the "cloister-crafts" of book-painting, ivory-carving, and metalwork; and it was by means of these portable objects, small in scale but precious in quality, that the iconographic tradition was inherited from the late-antique period, developed in the ninth—and still more in the tenth and eleventh—centuries, and so transmitted to the Romanesque age when monumental sculpture began again. The reasons for this predominance of the minor arts, as we have already noted, are partly practical, but partly also racial. Nomadic peoples do not develop monumental forms; and this instinct for mobility survived quite late into the Middle Ages in western Europe, where the stable social conditions necessary for the orderly development of monumental art hardly existed till the eleventh century. But apart from the influence which the material circumstances of life exerted upon the choice of artistic form in the early Middle Ages, the so-called "minor" or "applied" arts were naturally congenial to the northern mind; the Celts and the Germans had always exercised their ingenuity and inventiveness on the decoration of articles of everyday use, rather than upon independent objects for disinterested contemplation like the cult-statues and commemorative sculpture of the Mediterranean peoples. This explains why the whole tendency of ninth-century art, as we have studied it, is to destroy the Mediterranean conception of the body existing in space and to substitute for it the symbol lying on a surface. But this symbol is no longer the pure calligram of the Celtic miniaturist; it is the skilful reduction for medieval purposes of the humanist image invented in antiquity—man himself, with all his functions fully developed.

The humanism of antique art is taken over by the medieval artist for its expressive value, not for its power of creating an illusion.[1] The medieval attitude to the organisation of pictorial scenes required a sequence of shapes which could be read and interpreted like the characters of the written word, rather than a complex of forms which were sensuously self-evident at a single glance. We have seen already how the Carolingian artist was perpetually employed in breaking up the instantaneous dramatic moment of the classical picture into the temporal narrative episode of the medieval illustration; and how this involved the negation of the antique conception of space-depth and the substitution for it of a conception of surface-time inherited from the east, but translated into a European idiom. The ancient forms, created by sensuous perceptions—first of touch, and later of vision, were recomposed into a simplified and symbolised form regulated by conceptual standards. This concept of a shape distinct to the mental rather than

[1] Cf. Goldschmidt in *Vorträge der Bibliothek Warburg*, i. (1921–2), pp. 40 ff.

the physical eye is, of course, characteristic of all so-called "primitive" art; and in this respect early medieval art is "primitive" compared with antique art, just as the art of the twentieth century is "primitive" compared with the art of the nineteenth century. But just as the change in the art of our own time is due to a change of spiritual needs, and not to a decline of skill or mental degeneration, so the change from antique to medieval art was due to a change in the imaginative attitude to the tangible and visible world. In the early Middle Ages, as at the present day, two contradictory, yet complementary, instincts were at work; and the resulting object is produced by the tension between them. The first of these is a conviction of the reality of matter and the second is a conviction of the need to escape from this reality and not be dominated by it. The particular form of this tension in Nordic art is that conflict between *Sachlichkeit* (literally, *thingliness*) and *Expressionismus*, to which we have already alluded as the dominating factor in the development of the German genius. The former instinct appears in the determination to create a thing with a life of its own and not simply to imitate a living thing: to make something which shall be more real than what we call "reality". The latter instinct is expressed by the effort to make that thing more alive than the living thing that suggested it.

The realisation of these two instincts in Carolingian art is what makes it important: what saves it from archaism and sterility on the one hand, and makes it suggestive and pregnant with future growth on the other. The instinct for *Sachlichkeit* made Carolingian artists discard the imitative and negative elements in antique art: the illusion of space and the acceptance of accidental appearances. On the positive side, moreover, it was responsible for their insistence on the material of their art: the beauty of pigment in miniature-painting, quality of surface in ivory-carving or metalwork. The instinct for *Expressionismus* made them heighten the colours, quicken the rhythms, intensify the gestures; it induced them to sacrifice the time-space logic of the antique scene in favour of the time-surface metaphor of the medieval narrative. By what seems at first to be a curious paradox, the medieval artist borrowed from antique models the methods by which he transmuted the antique conception of form. He abandoned the rigid Celtic calligrams and the dense jungle of Germanic ornament for fluent and elegant narrative and rapid scrolls of acanthus and vine derived from the art of the Mediterranean world. But the paradox is more apparent than real. In the first place the medieval artist converted prose into poetry by the vehemence of his imagination; and in the second place the material on which he relied for his themes was not the purely Hellenic art of pre-Alexandrian Greece, but the mixed art, partly European, partly oriental, and partly barbarised, of the later Roman Empire, placed at the service of the Christian Church. The imperfect appreciation of these two facts will go far to explain why, although the importance of Carolingian art has always been recognised, its essence and influence have been so generally misrepresented. So long as it was supposed that the aesthetic achievements of the

Carolingian Renascence were purely derivative and preservative, the range and depth of their inspiring power over the Ottonian and the Romanesque imagination seemed unintelligible. So long as it was assumed that mimicry of the antique style was the chief aim of the medieval copyist, and that his deviations were due to incapacity, the vitality and originality of Carolingian art must have remained incomprehensible. But now that we realise that all art is in a sense derivative, and conversely that the origins of a style are aesthetically the least important thing about it, we are in a position to undertake the analysis of a work of art and to distinguish what is original in it from what is borrowed, and how that borrowed element was transformed by the genius of the artist and the circumstances in which he worked. The analysis of Carolingian art here attempted is extremely tentative. It avoids all detail that seemed external to the immediate purpose, which was to show how the medieval artist approached his antique material, what that material was like, and why it was converted by the northern imagination into something altogether fresh and independent. The conclusions reached may be modified in particular instances, but it is hoped that the method chosen may have avoided some previous misconceptions and indicated some profitable themes for future research.

BIBLIOGRAPHY

i. Books

BALDWIN BROWN (G.), The Arts in Early England. 1903 ff.

BALDWIN SMITH (E.), Early Christian Iconography, and a School of Ivory-carvers in Provence. 1918.

BERTAUX (E.), L'art dans l'Italie méridionale. 1904.

BIAGI (G.), Reproductions from Illuminated Manuscripts: 50 plates from MSS. in the R. Medicean Laurentian Library. 1914.

BIRCH (W. DE G.), The History, Art, and Palaeography of the Manuscript styled the Utrecht Psalter. 1876.

BOINET (A.), La miniature carolingienne. 1913.

BREASTED (J. H.), Oriental Forerunners of Byzantine Painting. 1924.

BRÖNDSTED (J.), Early English Ornament. 1924.

BRUNN-BRUCKMANN, Denkmäler der griechischen und römischen Skulptur. 1888 ff.

BUCHNER (M.), Einhard als Künstler. 1921.

Einhards Künstler- und Gelehrtenleben. 1922.

BULLE (H.), Untersuchungen an griechischen Theatern. 1928.

CALDERINI (G.), DOMASZEWSKI (A.), and PETERSEN (E.), Die Marcus-Säule. 1896.

CRESWELL (K. A. C.), Early Muslim Architecture, i. 1932.

DALTON (O. M.), Byzantine Art and Archaeology. 1911.

East Christian Art. 1925.

DELBRUECK (R.), Antike Porträts. 1912.

Die Consular-Diptychen. 1929.

Antike Porphyrwerke. 1932.

Spätantike Kaiserporträts. 1933.

DE WALD (E. T.), The Stuttgart Psalter. 1930.

The Utrecht Psalter. 1933.

DIEZ (E.) and DEMUS (O.), Byzantine Mosaics in Greece. 1931.

DÜTSCHKE (H.), Ravennatische Studien. 1909.

ÉBERSOLT (J.), La miniature byzantine. 1926.

Orient et Occident, i. 1928.

FERRI (S.), L'arte romana sul Reno. 1931.

L'arte romana sul Danubio. 1933.

FOCILLON (H.), L'art des sculpteurs romans. 1931.

FRANKL (P.), Frühmittelalterliche und romanische Baukunst. 1926.

FRIEDLÄNDER (P.), Johannes von Gaza und Paulus Silentiarius. 1912.

GOLDSCHMIDT (A.), Die Elfenbeinskulpturen aus der Zeit der karolingischen und sächsischen Kaiser, i. 1914.
German Illumination: i. The Carolingian Period. 1928.

HASELOFF (A.), Pre-romanesque Sculpture in Italy. 1930.
HEKLER (A.), Greek and Roman Portraits. 1912.

IPPEL (A.), Indische Kunst und Triumphalbild. 1929.

JONES (L. W.), and MOREY (C. R.), The Miniatures of the MSS. of Terence. 1931.

KEMMERICH (M.), Frühmittelalterliche Porträtplastik in Deutschland. 1909.
KOCH (H.), Römische Kunst. 1925.
KÖHLER (W.), Die karolingischen Miniaturen: Die Schule von Tours, i. 1932; ii. 1934.
KOLLWITZ (J.), Die Lipsanothek von Brescia. 1933.
KÖMSTEDT (R.), Vormittelalterliche Malerei. 1929.

LAISTNER (M. L.W.), Thought and Letters in Western Europe: A.D. 500–900. 1931.
LEHMANN-HARTLEBEN (K.), Die Trajanssäule. 1926.
LEITSCHUH (F. F.), Geschichte der karolingischen Malerei. 1894.
LEPRIEUR (P.), La période carolingienne. *In* MICHEL (A.), Histoire de l'art, I, i, pp. 321 ff. 1905.
L'ORANGE (H. P.), Studien zur Geschichte des spätantiken Porträts. 1933.

MACLER (F.), L'évangile arménien: édition phototypique du MS. no. 229 de la bibliothèque d'Etchmiadzin. 1926.
MARLE (R. VAN), La peinture romaine au moyen-âge. 1921.
Iconographie de l'art profane au moyen-âge et à la renaissance, i. 1931; ii. 1933.
MERTON (A.), Die Buchmalerei von Sankt-Gallen vom ix. bis zum xi. Jahrhundert². 1923.
MIGNE (J. P.), Patrologiae Cursus Completus: Latin series 1844–64; Greek series 1857–1912.
MILLAR (E. G.), The Lindisfarne Gospels. 1923.
Monumenta Germaniae Historica (MGH.), 1877 ff.
MOREY (C. R.), The Sarcophagus of Claudia Antonia Sabina (Sardis v. 1). 1924.

NOGARA (B.), Le Nozze Aldobrandine . . . e altre pitture antiche, etc. 1907.

OMONT (H.), Miniatures des plus anciens MSS. grecs de la Bibliothèque Nationale du vi^{e} au xive siècle. 1929.
OSTROGORSKY (G.), Studien zur Geschichte des byzantinischen Bilderstreites. 1929.

OVERBECK (J.), Die antiken Schriftquellen zur Geschichte der bildenden Künste bei den Griechen. 1868.

PANOFSKY (E.), Die Perspektive als symbolische Form. 1927.
PEIRCE (H.) and TYLER (R.), L'art byzantin, i. 1932; ii. 1934.
PFUHL (E.), Die Malerei und Zeichnung der Griechen. 1923.
Poetae Latini Aevi Carolini, ed. DÜMMLER (E.), i.1 881; ii. 1884. (PLAC.)

RAND (E. K.), A Survey of the MSS. of Tours. 1929.
RIEGL (A.), Spätrömische Kunstindustrie[2]. 1927.
RIZZO (G. E.), La pittura ellenistico-romana. 1929.
RODENWALDT (G.), Die Kunst der Antike. 1927.
ROSENBERG (M.), Zellenschmelz, iii. 1921.

SCHLOSSER (J. VON), Schriftquellen zur Geschichte der karolingischen Kunst. 1892.
SCHRAMM (P. E.), Die zeitgenossischen Bildnisse Karls des Grossen. 1928.
STETTINER (R.), Die illustrierten Prudentius-Handschriften. 1895, 1905.
STORNAJOLO (C.), Le miniature della topografia cristiana di Cosma Indicopleuste. 1908.
STRONG (E.), Apotheosis and After-Life. 1915.
Scultura romana, i. 1923; ii. 1926.
Art in Ancient Rome. 1928.
STRZYGOWSKI (J.), Origin of Christian Church Art. 1923.
Der Norden in der bildenden Kunst Westeuropas. 1926.

TOYNBEE (J. M. C.), The Hadrianic School. 1934.

VENTURI (A.), Storia dell' arte italiana, i. 1901; ii. 1902.

WESTWOOD (J.), The Bible of the Monastery of St. Paul near Rome. 1876.
WICKHOFF (F.) and HARTEL (R. VON), Die Wiener Genesis. 1895.
Roman Art (trans. and revis. by E. Strong). 1900.
WILPERT (J.), Römische Mosaiken und Malereien . . . vom iv-xiii Jahrhundert. 1917.
WÖLFFLIN, (H.) Kunstgeschichtliche Grundbegriffe. 1915 (transl. Hottinger. 1932).

ZIMMERMANN (H.), Vorkarolingische Miniaturen. 1916.

ii. *Periodicals (with abbreviations used in footnotes)*

AA.	= Archäologischer Anzeiger.
AJA.	= American Journal of Archaeology.
AM.	= Athenische Mitteilungen.
Bull. Com.	= Bulletino Comunale.
Burl. Mag.	= Burlington Magazine.
BZ.	= Byzantinische Zeitschrift.
GBA.	= Gazette des Beaux-Arts.

JdI. = Jahrbuch des Deutschen Archäologischen Instituts.
JHS. = Journal of Hellenic Studies.
Meded. = Mededeelingen des Nederlandsch Instituut . . . te Rome.
Mon. Piot = Fondation Eugène Piot: Monuments et Mémoires.
NGG. = Nachrichten der Göttinger Gesellschaft der wissenschaften.
Prussian Jahrbuch = Jahrbuch der Preussischen Kunstsammlungen.
RM. = Römische Mitteilungen.
Vienna Jahrbuch = Jahrbuch der Kunstsammlungen des allerhöchsten Kaiserhauses.

INDEX

THE END